ROMANTIC COCKTAILS ICON KEY

All of the drinks in this book were collected because they are inherently romantic or can be romantic based on the situation. To help you navigate all of the recipes, we have put together a series of icons to indicate what life and love events each of these beverages match. On first blush, some of the icons might not seem to match the drinks, but seriously, some breakups call for champagne. Flip through casually, or pick a theme—how you use it is up to you.

ICON	ROMANTIC OCCASION
♥	New love and crushes
➴ ➴	Jealousy, sour grapes
💔	Breakups and broken hearts
🥂	Celebrations, anniversaries, parties
💍	Engagements and weddings

Romantic

COCKTAILS

Romantic COCKTAILS

CRAFT COCKTAIL RECIPES
FOR COUPLES, CRUSHES,
AND STAR-CROSSED LOVERS

BY CLAIR MCLAFFERTY

ABRAHAM ROWE PHOTOGRAPHY

WHALEN
BOOK·WORKS

New York City

Romantic Cocktails

13-Digit ISBN: 9781732512610
10-Digit ISBN: 1732512612

This book may be ordered by mail from the publisher. Please include $5.99 for postage and handling.
Please support your local bookseller first!

Books published by Whalen Book Works are available at special discounts when purchased in bulk.
For more information, please email us at info@whalenbookworks.com.

Whalen Book Works
338 East 100 Street, Suite 5A
New York, NY 10029

www.whalenbookworks.com

Cover and interior design by Melissa Gerber
Typography Adobe Caslon, Adobe Garamond, Aphrodite Text, Aurora Regular,
Bell MT Regular, Brandon Grotesque, Eveleth, Gotham, and Pinto No_05 Swashes
Photography and styling by Abraham Rowe Photography
Portrait of Claire on page 218 by Meredith Ryncarz Photography,
with styling by Brittany Ann McNaughton of Forecast Salon

Printed in China
2 3 4 5 6 7 8 9 0

Recipes including raw eggs and raw seafood (not to mention alcohol) should be avoided by pregnant women, infants, the elderly, and anyone with an impaired immune system. Use caution with fire, alcohol, and feelings.

Dedication

To all the people who have helped
me relearn what it means to love
and be loved: This one's for you.

Contents

Introduction

Love is the Key

To find a cocktail to suit your mood,
see the Romantic Cocktails icon key
on the inside front cover of this book.

Flirtini, page 122

Romancing the
COCKTAIL

It is hard to define what, exactly, constitutes a romantic cocktail. It is not necessarily in the cost of the ingredients or the size of the garnish, although these things can add to the mood. Instead, a romantic cocktail derives its power from how it is chosen, made, and presented. Though wine is often associated with candlelit dinners, thoughtfully prepared cocktails can easily fill that role. A well-chosen tipple sets the tone for the evening, so do not hesitate to ask what your date or guests enjoy.

The most romantic drinks are ones thoughtfully chosen to match your partner, hopeful partner, or party's tastes. Putting a whiskey cocktail in front of an avowed vodka drinker may challenge them, but it can also clearly demonstrate that you do not know them. Instead, choose a cocktail similar to what they usually drink. If they adore **Old Fashioneds** (page 66), change up the bitters or whiskey in the recipe to make it your own. If they love **Daiquiris** (page 104), whip up a syrup in one of their favorite flavors just for them.

Herein, you will find romantic vintage cocktail recipes (page 28) and drinks that please the eye with their color and the senses with their flavors (page 88). But you will also discover mixtures that include ingredients thought to be aphrodisiacs (page 116), no-ABV cocktails to keep you sober for the most important nights (page 138), cocktails for two (page 152), and concoctions from bartenders who practice their craft at bars around the world (page 170). To help you navigate the intricacies of these drinks, I have put together instructions on homemade snacks and ingredients (page 190), and included a guide to make stocking your bar effortless (page 12). If you want to learn more about any of these ingredients, read **Knowledge Is Sexy** (page 20). The drinks in this book contain ingredients thought to be aphrodisiacs and have names related to aspects of love, even its loss. Each can be made for any occasion, but it is my hope that you will use these recipes to romance someone special.

—*Clair McLafferty*

The Well-Stocked Bar

What constitutes a well-stocked bar depends on the person stocking the bar as well as the people who will be using it. If your goal is to build a romantic bar for dating and general entertaining rather than for one other specific person, it may be most helpful to stock all of the basic liquors: brandy, gin, rum, tequila, vodka, and whiskey. Many subsets of these liquors exist, so where possible, recipes note what type of liquor to reach for next time you are at the store.

If you are setting up on a budget, start with what you like and are likely to drink. If you love tequila cocktails, buy a bottle for your house! Next, start to stock up on things for your lover (or lovers) and close friends. If they love rum, buy a bottle and keep ingredients for a simple single cocktail on hand. From there, fill out your liquor cabinet as you can.

For each bottle you buy, be prepared to spend around twenty to thirty dollars. Though it may be tempting to buy bottom-shelf liquors to fill your cabinets, spending just a few dollars more can yield a huge difference in quality in flavor—and in your quality of life the next day. If you ever want suggestions on what to buy, ask a bartender whose taste you trust.

Depending on where you are located, some of the more esoteric ingredients like crème de violette may be slightly more difficult to acquire. In many states, you may be able to order a bottle or two through your favorite liquor store. When in doubt, ask someone who works there.

If you are looking for premade cocktail ingredients, most grocery stores contain a section for mixers, typically located near the wine, beer, and soda. Even big-box retailers typically carry at least one brand of bitters (usually Angostura), along with simple syrup and premade freezer-ready cocktails.

Although you can buy simple syrup, it does not take much time, and costs very little to make at home (page 212). As a result, there is no reason to spend money on basic simple syrup. For other syrups like orgeat or grenadine, we have included recipes, but depending on the amount of time you have available to make these ingredients, it may be more convenient to purchase them. To make them from scratch, flip to page 190. If you invest the time to make your own syrups, **Limoncello** (page 210), or other homemade ingredients, consider making big batches once you have your recipes dialed in. With a printed label and recipe, bottled ingredients make great gifts, and can teach you how to tweak your home cocktail recipes until they are perfect.

Anywhere lemon or lime juice is mentioned, juice it fresh. The shelf-stable options at the grocery store are extremely convenient, but tend to contain stabilizers that add bitter flavors to the juice. These changes are noticeable, flavor-wise, in finished cocktails. If you are skeptical, make two **Daiquiris** (page 104) with the same syrup and rum, one with shelf-stable juice and one with fresh juice.

The good news is that a bowl of lemons and limes makes for a great centerpiece either on a counter or on a table. If you want your measurements to be ultra-precise and the flavors in your cocktails to be easily repeatable, strain out the pulp after juicing. When strained, these juices will stay good for about 48 hours from the time of juicing. Beyond that, they'll start to taste like the shelf-stable stuff.

Party Planning For a Crowd

If you are shopping for a party, there are some things you will want to keep on hand in your pantry.

. . . .

At the grocery store, grab some:

- ☐ Limes
- ☐ Lemons
- ☐ White sugar for syrups (page 25)
- ☐ Honey
- ☐ Ginger
- ☐ Soda water
- ☐ Ice
- ☐ Aromatic bitters, such as Angostura
- ☐ Orange bitters

When you hit the liquor store, pick up:

- ☐ Your favorite liquor
- ☐ One specialty bottle, such as Fernet-Branca or Chartreuse*
- ☐ Campari
- ☐ Aperol
- ☐ Maraschino cherries, such as Luxardo

*Fernet and Chartreuse may seem like esoteric ingredients to keep at your home, but they are a good indicator to bartenders and cocktail enthusiasts that you have some idea of how to mix cocktails. Both also work as flavorful straight shots, but also work in cocktails like the **Hanky Panky** (page 54), **Bijou** (page 40), or **Widow's Kiss** (page 83).

. . . .

The easiest way to entertain for a crowd is to make cocktails in advance. For tips and tricks of scaling up your favorite cocktail, check out page 23. If you would rather make a recipe that is already designed for a crowd, flip to Chapter 5: Drinks for Two on page 152 to check out drink recipes for two or more.

A Guide to Tools and Glassware

Having the right tools on hand means that you are one step closer to being prepared for any romantic moments that call for a drink. If you find yourself without your tools, there are ways to still make delicious beverages, as outlined on page 25, but a home bartending setup looks classy. To get started, you need a cocktail shaker, a jigger, a Hawthorne strainer, and either a mixing glass or pint glass paired with a mixing spoon.

TOOLS

Cocktail shakers come in three main styles: cobbler, Parisian, and Boston. Cobbler shakers are the most common type of shaker sold for home use. These have three parts, including a built-in strainer, but most do not seal well, so they are not often used at professional bars. However, they are perfectly suitable for home use. More commonly, you will see professionals shaking with a Bold Boston shaker (a combination of a pint glass and a larger metal tin) or a Bold Parisian shaker (two metal containers). I personally love Parisian shakers, but they can be difficult to seal or get unsealed once the drink is mixed.

Jiggers are simply small measuring tools used to measure liquid ingredients by volume. Some liquor brands include jiggers in promotional packaging, but these are not always consistent. In making drinks, this can mean that the recipe and the actual measurement you make do not match. Some online retailers such as Cocktail Kingdom (page 219) have quality-controlled products, but in the end, it is more important to enjoy the drink you make than to have perfect proportions.

A Hawthorne strainer will help to keep all but the smallest ice shards out of your finished cocktail. By straining and using fresh ice to serve, you will help to preserve the flavors in your drink from overdilution. Passable strainers are available almost anywhere bar tools are sold.

For stirred cocktails, a cut-glass mixing glass is a super sexy way to prepare a cocktail. However, the prettiest ones are often expensive, like the yarai pattern from Cocktail Kingdom. If you are bartending on a budget, try out a Mason jar or pint glass instead.

A punch bowl is always a lovely addition to any china cabinet, and is convenient for batching a large-format version of your favorite cocktail (Bigger Is Better, page 23) or a party-ready punch like the Champagne Punch (page 160).

GLASSWARE

Most recipes for cold drinks call for chilled glassware. To quickly chill glassware for single serving drinks, fill the glass with ice when you begin mixing the beverages. When the drink is ready, dump out the old ice and strain the cocktail into the chilled glass.

Champagne flutes are tapered, with a conical shape that holds between 6 to 10 ounces. Most, but not all, have stems. Many cocktails that contain sparkling wine are served in these glasses. Other wine glasses are sometimes used to serve sparkling wine, but other wines are not typically served in this glass.

A cocktail glass is a stemmed glass that is conical in shape and holds up to 10 ounces. A Martini glass is a subtype of cocktail glass used for many citrusy drinks that are not Martinis, but have been called such after the shape of the glass.

A Collins glass is a cylindrical glass that typically holds between 10 to 14 ounces. For many drinks, the glass is filled with ice, but for some egg drinks, it is served without.

The coupe glass is rumored to have been modeled after Marie Antoinette's breast, but unfortunately there is no historical evidence behind the claim. These glasses may be better known as a champagne coupe or saucer, but are more often used for citrusy tipples.

A **highball glass** is a type of tumbler that usually holds somewhere between 8 to 12 ounces, and is most often used for serving combinations of liquor and soda. Typically, these are taller than rocks glasses, but are shorter and wider than Collins glasses.

Julep cups are traditionally made from sterling silver or pewter to chill down juleps to frosty temperatures.

A **martini glass** is a subset of the cocktail glass. Most are stemmed glasses topped with an inverted conical bowl.

For cocktail use, **mugs** should be wide mouthed to allow alcohol vapor to dissipate instead of concentrate over the surface of the drink. To keep hot drinks warm for longer, fill the mug you will use to serve it with hot water when you are a few minutes away from serving, and then toss out the hot water right before pouring drinks into glasses. Like icing down glasses for cold drinks, this will help to keep hot drinks warmer for longer. Warm mugs are also quite pleasant to hold, especially on cold nights.

An **Old Fashioned glass** is another name for a rocks glass. These glasses typically hold 6 to 10 ounces, and were traditionally used as the vessel for stirred drinks like their namesake, the **Old Fashioned** (page 66).

Parfait glasses, or **goblets,** are tall, narrow glasses with short stems traditionally used to serve layered desserts known as parfaits.

A pint glass is a 16-ounce glass most recently used to serve beer, but that can also be used as a mixing glass.

Punch cups typically come in sets of four or more. They are smaller than most other glassware, and were traditionally used to further the communal experience of drinking punch.

Shot glasses are around $1^{1}/_{2}$ ounces, and were originally made to hold or measure straight liquor, but are typically used for serving drinks designed to be drunk as quickly as possible.

A sidecar is a glass served alongside a coupe or cocktail glass to hold any liquid from a recipe that did not fit in the proscribed vessel. Sidecars may also be used to serve small portions of liquid meant as a pairing or chaser.

A tiki mug is a large, ceramic mug that originated in a tiki bar restaurants. This term typically refers to glassware that portrays fantastical Polynesian-inspired imagery or other tropical themes.

A wine glass is a stemmed or unstemmed goblet-shaped glass used to served wine. Different glasses are sold to accentuate typical flavor profiles of different styles of wine, but a red-wine glass works well for drinking most types of wine, even sparkling.

Knowledge Is Sexy

Having a basic knowledge of common spirits is sexy. Here are the essentials for each.

Brandy is a liquor distilled from fruit that is often aged in oak barrels. Most, like **cognac**, **armagnac**, and **pisco** are made from grapes, but products made from other fruits, such as cherry, are labeled as fruit brandy. For cocktails, **Korbel**, **Ansac**, and **E&J** stand up well and will not break the bank. One exception is **calvados**, which is an apple brandy produced in a particular part of France. **Eau de vies** and **aquavits** are typically unaged brandies, and they tend to be somewhat fiery.

Within the United States, **gin** is defined as a liquor flavored with juniper. Juniper gives gin the piney flavor it is associated with. Four main types exist: **Old Tom**, which is typically sweetened to balance out the floral notes; **London dry**, the most familiar, juniper-heavy standard that, despite the name, can be produced anywhere; **Plymouth**, which is just like London dry, only it must be produced in Plymouth, England; and new wave, a category that encompasses the newer, more experimental gins. There is also **navy proof** gin, which is like London dry, but with a higher ABV. For most cocktails contained in this book, a London dry gin such as **Tanqueray** or **Broker's** will work just fine.

Rum is distilled from sugarcane or its by-products. It can be, and is, made all over the world, and the legal restrictions on it vary from country to country. Typically, it falls into one of three oversimplified, outdated categories: French, Spanish, or flavored. The delineations based on language are based on the countries that colonized the

Caribbean locales that actually produce rum. Each is sold as white (unaged or filtered), aged, or gold (typically unaged, but colored artificially). Styles of rum from French-speaking former colonies, such as **rhum agricole**, are made with fresh sugarcane juice, which results in a funky, slightly vegetal product. Former Spanish colonies often tend toward the more familiar clean, neutral style. Flavored rums tend to be sugary affairs with tropical flavors like coconut or spiced rums named after pirates or sea life. Cocktails that call for white rum will be served well with **Don Q Platino** or **Bacardi white**.

Tequila is distilled from blue Weber agave plants and must be produced in one of five states in Mexico. Always make sure to buy tequilas labeled as "100% de agave," as any others will be distilled from a mixture of at least 51 percent agave and sugar. Most tequilas will be classified by age as **blanco** or **plato** (silver), **reposado, añejo**, and **extra añejo**, but some producers also sell gold tequila. Though some gold tequilas are made by mixing aged tequila and unaged tequila, most are produced by adding artificial coloring. **Mezcal** may be made by distilling any strain of agave, but its production is also restricted to a few Mexican states.

Vodka can be made from anything organic with enough sugar to support fermentation as long as it is distilled to more than 90 percent alcohol by volume. Only about five percent of vodka is distilled from potatoes: the vast majority of the category is produced using grain, although some are made from milk. Vodkas tend to have subtle differences in flavor and texture, and drinkers who prefer it tend to have a favorite brand. If you're starting out, **Tito's** or **Ketel One** work well for making cocktails.

Whiskey (also spelled "whisky") is defined in most countries as a liquor distilled from grain that has been aged in barrels. **Bourbon** is a whiskey produced within the United States that is distilled from majority corn and aged in new oak barrels that also meets several other legal requirements. **Rye whiskey** is distilled from at least 51 percent rye and other grains and then is aged. **Scotch whisky** is distilled from malted barley or other grains and aged in previously used casks for at least three years. **Irish whiskey** is typically distilled from unmalted barley and aged. Conventionally, Irish and American products are spelled with an "e," while Canadian, Scotch, and Japanese labels spell it without. However, this rule is neither hard nor fast.

Don't Get Bitter

Bitters are a misunderstood part of the cocktail canon. They are made by steeping herbs in booze, and are used in small quantities. You might think a dash makes a whole drink bitter. In fact, it adds depth and complexity to a drink, and makes it taste less sweet.

Originally, bitters were a staple in doctors' medicine bags sold as cures for everything from dyspepsia to headaches. This practice changed with the Pure Food and Drug Act of 1906, which also established the Food and Drug Administration (FDA). This legislation prevented bitters being sold as medicine, which left Angostura as almost the only brand left standing. When Prohibition hit a few years later, most remaining brands shared the same fate. Today, bitters come in hundreds of flavors from dozens of brands: citrus, aromatic, fruit, grilling spices— even crawfish boil.

Bigger Is Better

Sometimes, size does matter. When hosting a party or other gathering, making a large, batched cocktail instead of spending the night making individual drinks can help you enjoy the event. Here are a few tips on scaling up single-serving beverages:

First, choose a fairly simple recipe. Anything with a muddled ingredient like mint or fruit will be tough to replicate on a large scale. Likewise, anything with dairy or egg white may result in textural issues or inconsistencies.

Once you have found a relatively simple recipe, multiply it by however many cocktails you want to make in total. So, if you want to make eight **Daiquiris**, you would multiply 2 ounces of rum, $^3/_4$ ounce fresh lime juice, and $^3/_4$ ounce simple syrup by 8. You would have 16 ounces, or two cups of rum, 6 ounces (or $^3/_4$ cup) lime juice, and 6 ounces (or $^3/_4$ cups) simple syrup.

However, this recipe does not account for the dilution added when shaking single cocktails, which typically works out to roughly $^1/_6$ cup per cocktail. To account for that, add $^1/_6$ cup chilled water for every serving, but back off just a bit if you plan to serve the drinks over ice, as the ice will melt as the party continues. For the Daiquiri punch, add 1 cup of ice-cold water and stir it all together.

One more thing: In larger versions of most cocktails, the citrus juice can become a bit overpowering, so begin with $^1/_2$ cup of juice and then add more to taste if it is too sweet. Thanks to the citrus juice, these batches will only stay good for two or so days if kept in the fridge, so drink up.

Batching stirred cocktails is an even easier proposition. When you are ready to make the batch, simply multiply the single-serving recipe by how many cocktails you want to make. If you are okay with stirring before serving, add ice and stir right before the party gets going or pour the undiluted batch into cups over ice 15 minutes before guests arrive. Or make your batch several hours in advance, adding $1/6$ to $1/8$ cup water per serving. Stir well and chill the whole pitcher in the fridge or freezer until chilly, about 1 to 2 hours.

A Note On Mistakes

As Bob Ross always said, a mistake is a happy little accident. But when you are making a drink it might not seem that way. Luckily, there are a couple ways to fix less-than-ideal outcomes.

If a drink is too bitter, add a tiny half pinch of salt. Saline brings out citrus flavors and makes the whole slightly brighter and sweeter.

If your cocktail is too sweet, throw in a dash of bitters. Trust that it will not make your drink bitter; instead, it will balance out the sweetness. If your drink makes it into the glass and it tastes too strongly of alcohol, pour it back into the shaker or mixing glass and shake or stir for 3 to 5 more seconds. Strain onto fresh ice, and taste it again. For desperate times when you run out of ice and need a shaken cocktail, add roughly $1/6$ ounce or $1/8$ ounce of cold water to the ingredients instead of ice and shake to combine. Or drink your booze straight. We will not judge you for it.

Are you short on equipment? Not all homes have a full bartending set-up. Luckily, you can use a shot glass instead of a jigger to measure simple drinks like the Daiquiri by proportion. If you still need to shake something, pour the ingredients back and forth between two cups with ice. To strain the mixture, use a whisk or, in desperate times, your fingers. But do not try that at a bar. Stirred cocktails can be made and stirred in Mason jars or even pint glasses rather than mixing glasses.

Unfortunately, there is no way to rescue a watered-down drink. You can try adding a bit more booze, but there is no shortcut to rescuing the drink—other than making it again or drinking faster next time.

The History and Mystique of Romantic Cocktails

It is hard to imagine any celebration of romantic milestones without a drink in hand. First dates, engagements, engagement parties, weddings, anniversaries, and vow renewals require toasts! Luckily, with **Zero-Proof Cocktails** (page 138), even non drinkers can feel included in the festivities. The most visible tipple for almost all of these occasions is champagne or another sparkling wine, but in times past, couples toasted with what was locally available. No matter if it was wine, cider, beer, *pulque* (a fermented agave beverage native to Mexico), there was a drink in hand.

Drinks requiring effort to prepare have long been associated with romance. Love potions have been a staple of fairy tales since time immemorial, with wicked—or well-meaning—characters trying to secure the affection of their beloved. Perhaps that is why so many foods have been assigned aphrodisiac qualities over the course of history (see **Love Potions**, page 116).

After 1693 in Europe, the drink of choice for the nobility would have been champagne in any form. But for celebrations, it may have been popularly served up in a punch-style drink that some cocktail historians think might have inspired the **French 75** (page 46). These parties were the height of elegance, and can be again with a bit of imagination. If bubbles are not your thing but you would still like to make drinks for a crowd, check out **Drinks for Two or More** (page 152) or flip to page 23 for tips on scaling up your favorite beverage.

There has always been a romance associated with a well-crafted beverage. Unlike food, which is made behind closed doors in a restaurant, beverages are poured or mixed in front of the person drinking them. It is a performance that builds the anticipation of actually getting to experience the beverage itself.

The origins of many of the classic cocktails this book are lost to history. Though American Prohibition is still a popular party theme, it pushed many bartenders into different fields or into bartending abroad, and it created a break in the oral traditions that bartenders pass down from generation to generation. Thanks to the internet and renewed interest in cocktails and bartenders, the origins of modern drinks are easier to trace. Their visibility has also led to a rise in signature cocktails becoming a part of many wedding celebrations. Though some are simple juice and booze, others are more complex mixtures of bespoke ingredients. For some beautiful ideas to get you started on your own, flip to **Pretty Drinks** on page 88, or for timeless ideas, check out **Vintage Romance** on page 28. Modern romantic concoctions also make use of flavors not traditionally used in drinks, like the oyster shells in the **Oyster Shell Martini** (page 128) or new combinations of flavors like the brown butter–washed rum in the **Larry's Homework** (page 182). To look at other modern cocktails, take a turn in **Modern Craft Cocktails** on page 170. Though many of the ingredients for contemporary cocktails require advance preparation, being able to talk about the energy and care put into making the ingredients for the drink goes above and beyond. Is there anything more romantic?

CHAPTER 1:

Vintage Romance

Everything looks more glamorous in sepia tones, and romance is no exception. Luckily, the world of vintage cocktail recipes offers no shortage of cocktails that have romantic names, recipes, and hail from what some would call simpler times. Thanks to the passage of time, the origin stories of many of these drinks are murky at best and completely lost to history at worst. Wherever they came from, each of these tipples stands the test of time. Check out the sexy lineup of recipes ranging from spirit-forward pre-Prohibition cocktails like the **Adonis** (page 32) and the **Old Fashioned** (page 66), to sippable Hollywood staples including the **Stinger** (page 69) and **Mojito** (page 64).

hunky

ADONIS

This cocktail is named for an 1884 Broadway burlesque musical rather than the the original Adonis, who was the mortal lover of the Greek goddess Aphrodite. Its brawn comes from its gorgeous flavors rather than a high-proof composition. Thanks to its relatively low ABV, it is also great for marathon drinking sessions.

2 ounce dry oloroso sherry*
1 ounces sweet vermouth
2 dashes orange bitters
Orange peel, for garnish

Stir sherry, sweet vermouth, and orange bitters with ice in a mixing glass. Strain into a chilled cocktail or wine glass. Express the orange peel over the surface of the drink by squeezing it with the colorful side toward the surface of the drink.

Oloroso sherry tends to be dry, dark, and nutty, and is the base for many of the sweet sherries sold within the United States and abroad—such as cream sherries.

a liquid love letter

AIRMAIL

Slow down the world for a few minutes with an Airmail to a time when every missive professing long-distance love took days to arrive. Deliver with care, and most of all, enjoy the luxurious citrus flavors and the bubbles fizzing over your tongue.

2 ounces gold rum, such as Appleton

³/₄ ounce **Honey Syrup** (page 213)

³/₄ ounce fresh lime juice

Champagne, to top

Straw, for garnish

Lime or orange twist, for garnish

Shake rum, honey syrup, and lime juice with ice. Strain into a Collins glass full of ice. Top with champagne, and garnish with straw and lime twist.

"More than kisses, letters mingle souls."
—*John Donne*

bee mine

BEE'S KISS

Honey is a symbol of fertility in some cultures. The origin of the word "honeymoon" is thought to have stemmed from the practice of drinking mead, or fermented honey, during the first month or so of a new marriage. But watch out for the sting—this tipple carries a goodly bit of gin underneath its sweetness and creaminess. The Bee's Kiss is perfect as a nightcap or dessert, especially when curled up next to your honey on a chilly fall night.

2 ounces white rum
3/4 ounce heavy cream
3/4 ounce **Honey Syrup**
(page 213)

Shake white rum, heavy cream, and honey syrup vigorously with ice until cold. Strain into a chilled coupe glass.

so groovy

THE BEE'S KNEES

Tell your honey they are the best by serving them a Bee's Knees. This slang term, which originated as a phrase meaning that something was nonsensical, had, by Prohibition, morphed into a phrase designating that something was excellent. The second definition is the one that has stuck around, so this wonderful little drink can be a compliment and a beverage order all in one.

2 ounces gin
³/₄ ounce **Honey Syrup** (page 213)
³/₄ ounce lemon juice
Lemon wheel, for garnish

Shake gin, honey syrup, and lemon juice with ice. Garnish with a lemon wheel.

A Simple Variation
Substitute white rum for gin to make a **Princess**.

BETWEEN THE SHEETS

This Sidecar variation won't spill the beans on your pillow talk last night, but it might have you revealing more than you bargained. The combination of rum and cognac bring together a slightly sweeter flavor profile than the original Sidecar, but the citrusy notes are present in both.

¾ ounce rum

¾ ounce cognac

¾ ounce orange liqueur, such as Cointreau

¾ ounce fresh lemon juice

Lemon twist, for garnish (optional)

Shake rum, cognac, orange liqueur, and lemon juice well with ice. Strain into a chilled cocktail glass. Garnish with a twist, if desired.

A Simple Variation
To make the original recipe, a **Sidecar**, replace rum with cognac.

"Love is a smoke rais'd with the fume of sighs / Being purg'd, a fire sparkling in a lover's eyes."

—*Shakespeare,* Romeo & Juliet

vexing, but tasty

BIJOU

The name, which translates from the French to "jewel," is thought to have been inspired by the jewel-tone colors of each of the ingredients: diamond-hued gin, ruby-red vermouth, and emerald-green Chartreuse. Together, like any good relationship, they form flavors that are more than the sum of their parts.

1 ½ ounce gin
½ ounce sweet vermouth
½ ounce green Chartreuse
Lemon twist
Maraschino cherry,
such as Luxardo*

Mix gin, sweet vermouth, and Chartreuse with ice in a mixing glass. Strain into a chilled coupe or cocktail glass and garnish with a lemon twist and cherry.

*Before Prohibition, **maraschino cherries** were made by soaking tart marasca cherries in sugar syrup or liquor. Thanks to the temperance movement, producers began looking for ways to make them without booze and turned to chemicals like sulfur dioxide and calcium chloride to bleach the cherries and make them shelf-stable, then in a mixture of artificial food coloring, sugar, and other ingredients to color them a venomous neon red. Luxardo and other craft maraschino cherries return to the original tradition.

sophisticated

CHAMPAGNE JULEP

Champagne and mint are a heady combination, and with a bit of simple syrup and whiskey to tie the drink together, this cocktail transcends the sum of its parts. Though it is simply a Mint Julep with champagne substituted for bourbon, it is simple perfection when made well.

3 ounces champagne

½ ounce whiskey

¼ ounce **Simple Syrup** (page 212)

6 to 7 mint leaves

Mint sprig, for garnish

Add simple syrup to a julep cup. Gently press mint leaves into syrup until you can smell the mint. Add whiskey and champagne, then gently add a bit of crushed ice. Stir very gently. Add more ice and garnish with a mint sprig and a straw.

EASY DOES IT

When muddling delicate herbs like mint, be careful not to smash the mint to smithereens. Doing so releases chlorophyll, which is bitter, earthy, and unpleasant. Instead, lightly press the herb against the side of the glass with a muddler or wooden spoon until you can smell the mint. At this point, you have released the oils and are good to go. But if you are muddling fruit, go hard: you are trying to release the juice and the oils in the peel, and that requires more strength.

pop the champs

CHAMPAGNE COCKTAIL

The Champagne Cocktail is a simple mixture of sugar, bitters, and champs—which means it is almost an Old Fashioned, but with no dilution and champagne instead of whiskey. It is cool, collected, and brings all of the fizzy feelings of new romance to the table with endless possibilities for variations.

1 sugar cube
3 dashes aromatic bitters, such as Angostura
Champagne
Extra long twist of lemon peel

Place sugar cube in a champagne flute. Dash bitters over the cube to soak it. Fill glass slowly with champagne. Garnish with the lemon twist.

YOU CAN HAVE WHATEVER YOU LIKE

The Champagne Cocktail is easy to build, and is comprised of only three basic ingredients. As a result, it is infinitely customizable. If you want to make a more floral cocktail, substitute lavender or other herbal bitters for the Angostura. For a more citrusy take, substitute two dashes of lemon or orange bitters for two dashes of the Angostura. Even the choice of champagne can have a big impact on the resulting cocktail. A sweeter wine will obviously result in a sweeter drink, while a drier one will highlight more from the bitters and citrus. Beyond the liquid ingredients, the garnish can also be changed depending on the occasion. For a fruitier take, switch out the lemon peel for a few raspberries or blackberries. If you are feeling sassy, garnish instead with a piece of candy or a chocolate-covered strawberry, raspberry, or other fruit. To amp up the fire power and to get a step closer to a cocktail like the **French 75** (page 46), slip in ¹/₂ ounce of brandy or gin.

did it hurt when you fell from heaven?

FALLEN ANGEL

Obvious pickup lines aside, the Fallen Angel is a tart, slightly minty cocktail that brings together seemingly incompatible ingredients to make a tasty drink. Serve this up for lunch dates by making a couple and carry them in a flask for a perfect picnic.

2 ounces dry gin
½ ounce fresh lime juice
1 dash aromatic bitters, such as Angostura
2 dashes white crème de menthe*
Mint sprig, for garnish

Shake cognac or gin, lime juice, bitters, and crème de menthe with ice and strain into a chilled cocktail glass. Garnish with a sprig of mint.

Crème de menthe is a mint-flavored liqueur that comes in white and green. The two types are similar, flavor-wise, but the green has color added. For recipes like this one where the color is delicate, use white.

"The heart was made to be broken."
—*Oscar Wilde*

the heavy artillery

FRENCH 75

Though the French 75 is named after a style of cannon, the drink has become iconic for celebrations and romantic evenings. Clean, refreshing, and beautiful, this cocktail does kick like a cannon if you have one (or two) too many.

1 ½ ounces cognac or gin
½ ounce **Simple Syrup** (page 212)
½ ounce fresh lemon juice
Sparkling wine, to top
Lemon twist, for garnish

Shake gin, simple syrup, and lemon juice with ice. Strain into a chilled flute, top with sparkling wine, and garnish with a lemon twist.

Simple Variations

For a **French 95**, substitute bourbon for gin. For a **Crowd:** The French 75 is a great welcome cocktail for any celebration or dinner party. To make four at once, combine 1 cup cognac or gin, ⅓ cup simple syrup, and ¼ cup lemon juice. Add ⅓ cup of water, and stir well to combine. Chill in the fridge until you are ready to serve, and pour into glasses. Top with sparkling wine.

legendary

GIMLET

Though it was originally made with lime cordial, the formulation of most commercially available cordial has changed over time into a sugary, artificially flavored concoction. For a livelier and more romantic take, this recipe uses fresh lime juice and simple syrup. From Betty Draper's **Vodka Gimlet** in *Mad Men* to Raymond Chandler, this drink's glamorous history includes plenty of screen time.

2 ounces gin
³/₄ ounce **Simple Syrup**
(page 212)
³/₄ ounce fresh lime juice
Lime wheel, for garnish

Shake gin, simple syrup, and lime juice with ice. Strain into a chilled coupe glass and garnish with a lime wheel.

A Simple Variation
For a **Vodka Gimlet**, substitute vodka for gin.

"Of all the gin joints in all the towns in all the world, she walks into mine."
—*Casablanca*

demure, but fierce

MAIDEN'S PRAYER COCKTAIL

This cocktail is not a wilting flower, even if it takes its name from a popular 19th-century piece of music with approximately the same name. The gin you use will determine how assertive the piney juniper flavor is, but the drink as a whole will be tart and dry, in the best way possible.

1 ½ ounces gin
½ ounce orange liqueur, such as Cointreau
½ ounce fresh lemon juice
½ ounce fresh orange juice
Lemon twist, for garnish

Shake gin, orange liqueur, lemon juice, and orange juice well with ice. Strain into a chilled cocktail glass and garnish with a lemon twist.

jack be nimble

JACK ROSE

Whether named for a hit man or a bartender, this New Jersey cocktail keeps swinging. The rich, aged apple brandy gives the kick behind this one, while the grenadine and citrus work to round out the apple flavors into something nice. If you are looking for an easy cocktail to serve with a creamy or sharp cheese, this is it.

2 ounces applejack
1/2 ounce fresh lemon juice
1/2 ounce fresh lime juice
1/2 ounce **Grenadine** (page 213)
Lemon twist, for garnish (optional)

Shake applejack, lemon juice, lime juice, and grenadine with ice and strain into a chilled cocktail glass. Garnish with a lemon twist, if desired.

bittersweet

GOOD NIGHT KISS

Some nights call for a dessert drink that brings some bitterness along with the sweet. If tonight is one of those for you, this drink brings the bubbliness of a first kiss and the bite of parting at the door. It is a nightcap perfect for a night that you do not want to end.

1 dash Angostura
1 sugar cube
4 ounces champagne
1 ounce Campari

Dash Angostura bitters onto the sugar cube and drop into a champagne flute. Add champagne, and top with Campari.

"Good night, good night! Parting is such sweet sorrow, that I shall say good night till it be morrow."
—*William Shakespeare*, Romeo and Juliet

HANKY PANKY

On nights where shenanigans are on the menu, reach for your bottle of fernet. If you have a taste for the secret mix of herbs that makes up Fernet-Branca, you are bound to love the Hanky Panky. This saucy concoction has its roots in the legendary American Bar in London's Savoy Hotel.

1 ½ ounces gin
1 ½ ounces sweet vermouth
2 dashes Fernet-Branca
Orange peel or twist,
for garnish

Stir gin, sweet vermouth, and fernet in a mixing glass with ice until chilled, about 30 seconds. Strain into a chilled coupe glass. Squeeze an orange peel or twist over the glass and drop it in.

"Candy is dandy, but liquor is quicker."

—*Ogden Nash,* Hard Lines

HAVE A HEART

Keeping it classy when things get rough can be tough, but a boozy, tart, slightly funky beverage may be just what the doctor ordered.

1 ½ ounces gin
¾ ounces Swedish punsch*
¾ ounces fresh lime juice
¼ ounce **Grenadine** (page 213)
Lime wedge, for garnish

Shake gin, punsch, lime juice, and grenadine with ice, and strain into a chilled cocktail glass. Garnish with a lime wedge.

*Swedish Punsch is a funky ingredient more commonly known as punsch. Its roots are in a punch mixed from arrack, sugar, citrus, and blended with other rums that was served immediately. It was first sold as a premixed product in 1840, was first mixed in cocktails when it made it to the United States, but was sidelined by Prohibition. Almost a century later, it has been revived by the craft cocktail movement. KRONAN produces a good one, and it is available in most states.

"I have not broken your heart—you have broken it; and in breaking it, you have broken mine."

—*Emily Brönte*, Wuthering Heights

Skewer a raspberry
and a thin lime wheel
for a special garnish.

for starry-eyed lovers

HONEYMOON

This cocktail comes on strong, like new love, and mellows out into something funky but beautiful. With a name like this, it is perfect as a post-wedding tipple or a send-off toast for newlyweds.

2 ounces bonded apple brandy, such as Laird's
½ ounce orange curaçao
¼ ounce Bénédictine
½ ounce fresh lemon juice
Lemon twist, for garnish

Shake apple brandy, orange curaçao, Bénédictine, and lemon juice with ice and strain into a chilled coupe glass. Express the lemon twist over top and drop in.

Try a lemon wheel instead of a twist for a different look.

ninth time's the charm

LOVE POTION #9

We may not know what happened to the first eight potions, but this one is sure to inspire a bit of romance. In Greek mythology, strawberries originated as Aphrodite's tears over her lover's death. Thanks to their vitamin C content, they are still considered aphrodisiacs.

Lemon wedge
2 tablespoons sugar,
for rimming
1 1/2 ounce vodka
1/2 ounce peach schnapps
3 ounces grapefruit juice
Strawberry slice, for garnish

Use lemon wedge to rim martini glass with sugar. (See **Rimmed Glassware** on page 217 for a how-to.) Shake vodka, peach schnapps, and grapefruit juice with ice, and strain into the glass. Garnish with a strawberry slice perched on the rim of the glass.

"I will show you a love potion without drug or herb, or any witch's spell; if you wish to be loved, love."

—*Charles Lindberg*

Tahitian for "good"

MAI TAI

It is tart, sweet, and tastes like a tiny slice of a rummy tropical paradise. Unlike more modern cocktails made under the same name with a bunch of fruit juice, the original recipe is simple and nutty, while still maintaining a bit of mystery and funk. It is a favorite to include in tropical destinations in movies, sipped on screen in projects ranging from 1961's *Blue Pacific* to the modern day *Mad Men*. And it is good for any time you want to set a romantic tropical scene, whether at a summer party or on a bleak day in the depths of January.

1 ounce aged rum
½ ounce rhum agricole
½ ounce gold rum
½ ounce orange curaçao
1 ounce fresh lime juice
¾ ounce orgeat*
Umbrella and lime wheel or spent lime shell, for garnish
Sprig of mint, for garnish (optional)

Shake rums, orange curaçao, lime juice, and orgeat with ice until chilled. Strain into a rocks glass full of crushed ice and garnish with an umbrella and lime wheel. Alternately, garnish with a spent lime shell (what's left over when the juice is squeezed out) and a sprig of mint.

Orgeat is a tropical syrup made with almond milk, lime zest, and orange flower water. If you want to make it from scratch, check out the recipe on page 214. But Trader Vic's, Small Hand Foods, Giffard, and B. G. Reynolds all make good syrups as well.

Three Way

The Mai Tai can be made from only one
type of rum, but it is greatly improved by
using all three. Each of these three styles
of rum brings different flavors to the drink:
The aged rum brings oak and vanilla,
while the rhum agricole adds funk and
green earthiness that is balanced by the
sweetness of the gold.

refreshing and minty

MOJITO

As one of Bond's non-Martini drinks in *Die Another Day*, this cocktail is as recognizable as it is simple and delicious. Drink them on the beach or fantasize about more tropical times on your patio. Be careful to only lightly tap your mint: muddling it vigorously releases chlorophyll, the compound responsible for grassy, bitter Mojitos.

2 sprigs mint
Whole lime, quartered
2 ounces white rum
½ ounce **Simple Syrup**
(page 212)
Soda water, to top
Lime wheel, to garnish

Add mint sprigs to a Collins glass. Lightly press the mint against the side of the glass with a muddler. Add lime pieces, and muddle to release juice, then add rum and simple syrup and stir. Fill glass with ice, top with soda water, stirring gently to combine. Garnish with a lime wheel.

"Mojito? You should try it."
—*James Bond to Jinx*, Die Another Day

call me old fashioned

ORIGINAL OLD FASHIONED

Sometimes, the old ways are best. Mixing an Old Fashioned is one of them. It is just whiskey, bitters, sugar, and water, but it can come together to make something magical.

2 ounces rye whiskey

Heavy 1 teaspoon **Demerara Syrup*** (page 212)

2 dashes aromatic bitters, such as Angostura

1 dash orange bitters

Lemon twist, for garnish

Stir whiskey, demerara syrup, and both bitters with ice. Strain into a chilled rocks glass over one big cube. Garnish with a twist of lemon.

THE GOOD OLD DAYS

To get to the heart of the Old Fashioned, we first have to take a look at the Whiskey Cocktail, a simple concoction of bitters, sugar, spirit, and water that followed the first known written definition of a cocktail that was published in 1806. Over time, the cocktail got dressed up with fancy liqueurs like absinthe and maraschino liqueur into the Improved Whiskey Cocktail. But as with all good things, some people just wanted to drink the way they had in years past, and they called for an Old Fashioned Whiskey Cocktail. The spelling and punctuation of the name varied, but was eventually shortened to its current name.

new hotness

NEWER OLD FASHIONED

This fruit-heavy version may be more familiar to some. It is still pretty simple, but the addition of fruit brings it closer to another genre of classic cocktail: the Cobbler. If you are on the fence about Old Fashioneds, take both recipes for a spin and taste them side by side for your next date night. For bonus points, put together a **Cheese Board** (page 196), and see which recipe pairs better with which cheeses.

Sugar cube
2 dashes aromatic bitters, such as Angostura
Orange wedge
2 ounces bourbon whiskey, divided
Maraschino cherry, such as Luxardo, for garnish

Muddle the sugar, bitters, and orange wedge well in an old fashioned glass until sugar is mostly dissolved. Add $^1/_2$ ounce of the whiskey, and stir to further dissolve. Fill glass with ice, and add the rest of the whiskey. Stir gently, and drop the cherry in.

FRESH AND FRUITY

Fruit came a bit later in the Old Fashioned, but by the end of Prohibition, many Old Fashioneds arrived sporting a muddled orange slice and cherry. Since the beginning of the new era of cocktails, both the muddled fruit version and the austere original still remain on many, many menus.

very forward

PINK GIN

The beautiful color of this drink belies its potency. It is easy to see why Pink Gin was a favorite of the British Royal Navy in its heyday, as bitters were the treatment for most stomach ailments, and, well, gin cures all. Though its original use was decidedly unsexy, the color is a pale, delicate pink—perfect for mending hearts or breaking them all over again. To find your perfect balance of botanicals and bitters, start with three dashes and add more as needed.

2 ounces juniper-forward gin, such as Plymouth

3 to 6 dashes of bitters, such as Angostura*

Stir gin and bitters with ice until well chilled and strain into a chilled coupe glass.

*The bitters give this drink its pink color. Angostura and other dark red bitters work best for the drink's signature look and taste.

so minty fresh and so clean

STINGER

This posh drink was a favorite for pilots back in the 1940s. Despite its uncertain origins, it has gotten time on the silver screen, most notably when Cary Grant calls for one in *Kiss Them For Me*. It also makes a fabulous liquid dessert.

1 sprig mint, with 1 leaf reserved for garnish
2 ounces cognac
3/4 ounce crème de menthe
1 dash orange bitters

Lightly bruise mint in a cocktail shaker until you can smell the mint. Add cognac, crème de menthe, and bitters, and shake to combine. Strain into a chilled coupe glass and float the mint leaf on the surface of the drink.

Simple Variations
Add 2 to 3 dashes of Angostura bitters and garnish with a twist of lemon for a **Brant**. Substitute rum for brandy to make a **Picador**.

red-carpet dreamin'

ROYAL ROMANCE

Named for its birthplace, the Royal Hawaiian Hotel in Honolulu, this dreamy cocktail will have you feeling like royalty taking a beach vacation. The orgeat gives it a bit of floral and nutty flavor, while the lemon juice helps to bring down the sweetness just a bit. Float an edible flower on top, if desired, and garnish with a twist.

1 ½ ounces gin
1 ounce pineapple juice
½ ounce fresh lemon juice
¼ ounce orgeat*
Edible flower, for garnish (optional)
Lemon twist, for garnish (optional)

Shake gin, pineapple juice, lemon juice, and orgeat with ice and strain into a small cocktail glass. Garnish with an edible flower and a twist, if desired.

Orgeat is a tropical syrup made with almond milk, lime zest, and orange flower water. If you want to make it from scratch, check out the recipe on page 214. Orgeat can be labor-intensive, and even the most well-intentioned efforts can end up with a cloudy syrup. For a slightly easier approach, start with an unfiltered, unprocessed almond milk in the recipe. If you want to put your own spin on it, start with cashew or another nut milk instead of almond. But Trader Vic's, Small Hand Foods, Giffard, and B. G. Reynolds all make good syrups as well.

"My tastes are simple: I am easily satisfied with the best."

—*Winston Churchill*

The blue Asiatic Dayflower used here is a wild edible common in backyards and gardens. For more on garnishing drinks with flowers, see page 177.

well, that's forward

SEX ON THE BEACH

The Sex on the Beach is one of a slew of cocktails that rose to fame in the '80s and '90s that features a raunchy name and a bunch of sweet ingredients. Other familiar mainstays in this category include the Sex with an Alligator; Buttery Nipple; Blow-Job Shot; Long, Slow Comfortable Screw against the Wall; and many, many others too risqué to list here. Recipes for many of these drinks vary regionally, possibly because a bartender heard a catchy cocktail name while traveling and made up their own recipe to fit it when they got home. If you are having a night where you need turn the volume up to 11 and are unafraid, reach for the ingredients for a Sex on the Beach.

1 ½ ounce vodka
½ ounce peach schnapps
1 ounce orange juice or
pineapple juice
1 ounce cranberry juice
Orange wheel or pineapple
wedge, for garnish
Maraschino cherry,
for garnish (optional)

Shake vodka, schnapps, and both juices well with ice. Strain into a Collins glass filled with fresh ice. Garnish with an orange wheel or pineapple wedge, and, if desired, a cherry.

"Good sex is like good bridge. If you don't have a partner, you'd better have a good hand."

—*May West*

heavenly

SEVENTH HEAVEN

Heaven is a place on Earth wherever love lives. This cocktail is heavy on the botanicals, with the nutty maraschino and bitter grapefruit coming in as auxiliary flavors. It is strange and a bit bitter, just like heaven might be, and definitely like love is.

Sprig of mint, one leaf reserved for garnish

2 ounces gin

1/2 ounce maraschino liqueur, such as Luxardo

1/2 ounce fresh grapefruit juice

Gently press mint leaves in a cocktail shaker with a muddler or wooden spoon. Add gin, maraschino liqueur, grapefruit juice, and ice and shake. Strain into a chilled cocktail glass, and garnish with another mint leaf.

(For tips on muddling see **Easy Does It**, page 41.)

"Death and love are the two wings that bear the good man to heaven."

—*Michelangelo*

SOOTHER

It is forward, kind of weird, and definitely tastes like what it is: a strong, tart drink. Soothing indeed, but be sure to soothe your woes in moderation with this approach—it will sneak up on you quickly.

1 ounce cognac
1 ounce Jamaican rum
½ ounce orange curaçao
½ ounce fresh lemon juice
1 teaspoon apple juice
Lemon twist, for garnish

Shake cognac, rum, curaçao, lemon juice, and apple juice with ice, and strain into a goblet. Garnish with the lemon twist.

"The very winds whispered in soothing accents, and maternal Nature bade me weep no more."

—*Mary Shelley*

luxurious and silky soft

SOYER AU CHAMPAGNE (SILK WITH CHAMPAGNE)

This drink's name translates from the French as "Silk with Champagne"—a name with it lives up to with gusto. Though two dashes each of liqueur, juice, and brandy do not sound like a lot, together they add up to a soft, sweet base for the champagne. With the vanilla ice cream, the drink gains a rich, sensuous texture. But all together, this drink is as luxurious as drinking champagne while lying on cool silk sheets.

2 tablespoons
vanilla ice cream

2 dashes maraschino liqueur

2 dashes pineapple juice

2 dashes orange curaçao

2 dashes brandy

Champagne

Scoop ice cream into a parfait glass, and pour maraschino liqueur, pineapple juice, curaçao, and brandy over top. Fill with champagne, and garnish with a straw. Serve with a spoon.

"Pleasure without Champagne is surely artificial."
—*Oscar Wilde*

strong

TREMBLEMENT DE TERRE (EARTHQUAKE)

Love can hit you like an earthquake, which is what this drink's name translates to from the French. When it knocks you down, stir up this drink. Strong in flavor and proof, it might even keep you comfortable while you are rebuilding.

2 ½ ounces cognac
½ ounce absinthe
Lemon twist, for garnish

Stir cognac and absinthe in a mixing glass with ice. Strain into a chilled cocktail glass and garnish with a lemon twist.

"It is not light that we need, but fire; it is not the gentle shower, but thunder. We need the storm, the whirlwind, and the earthquake."

—*Frederick Douglass*

be a star

TUXEDO

Few things are as posh as the Ritz in Paris, so it is not surprising that a sexy but slightly strange Martini variation came out of it. The little bit of sweetness from the maraschino and anisette bring out some of the interesting herbal notes in the gin and vermouth here for quite the effect.

2 ounces gin
1 ounce dry vermouth
2 dashes maraschino liqueur
2 dashes of anisette,
such as Pernod

Stir gin, dry vermouth, maraschino liqueur, and anisette with ice and strain into a chilled martini glass.

"In a tuxedo, I'm a star.
In regular clothes, I'm a nobody."
—*Dean Martin*

it's complicated

THE WIDOW'S KISS

Watch out for this widow—one kiss can bring you to your knees. Outside of the calvados, each ingredient is heavily herbal. On paper, they may not appear to mesh. In practice, the combination is heady, herbaceous, and lingering. Proceed with caution.

1 ½ ounces Calvados*

¾ ounce green Chartreuse**

¾ ounce Bénédictine

2 dashes aromatic bitters, such as Angostura

Maraschino cherry

Shake Calvados, Chartreuse, Bénédictine, and bitters with ice and strain into a cocktail glass. Garnish with a cherry.

*Calvados is an apple brandy produced in Normandy, France. Though it can be made with a limited amount of pears, most producers avoid their use. Some of it is fiery eau-de-vie, but like cognac, some products are refined, cask-aged beauties.

Green Chartreuse is an intense, high-proof herbal liqueur that is naturally colored green from the infusion of 130 herbs and plants that go into its proprietary recipe. Its price tag also packs a punch, but a bottle of it will serve as a long-term investment in a home bar. **Bijou (page 40) is another exquisite charteuse cocktail to try.

a secret agent's drink

VESPER MARTINI

Since James Bond ordered this Martini variation in Ian Fleming's first Bond book, *Casino Royale*, it and its derivatives have arguably become synonymous for sophistication. The Vesper is also named for Bond's knockout companion, making it a necessary addition to the pantheon of romantic cocktails.

....

3 ounces gin
1 ounce vodka
½ ounce Kina Lillet, to taste
Lemon peel, to garnish

Stir gin, vodka, and Kina Lillet with ice in a mixing glass. Strain into a chilled coupe glass, and garnish with a lemon peel.

....

a second chance

ZOMBIE

After Donn Beach of Don the Beachcomber fame invented this drink, it became a legend with a limit. Each customer could only have two out of caution for its potency. The base ingredients require some advance preparation, and will likely require a dash to the liquor store, but the Zombie can be a good distraction from love lost—or bring you back to life from a hangover.

1 ½ ounces Jamaican rum

1 ½ ounces white rum

1 ounce 151-proof rum

½ ounce grapefruit juice

¼ ounce **Cinnamon Syrup** (page 212)

½ ounce Velvet Falernum*

¾ ounce fresh lime juice

¼ ounce **Grenadine** (page 212)

2 dashes absinthe

1 dash aromatic bitters, such as Angostura

Mint sprig, for garnish

Shake all three rums, grapefruit juice, cinnamon syrup, falernum, lime juice, grenadine, absinthe, and bitters with ice. Strain into a tiki mug over crushed ice. Garnish with a mint sprig by slapping it overtop the drink and then inserting it, stem first, by the straw next to the wall of the glass so that the bouquet (leaves) are above the surface of the drink. Go crazy with additional garnishes, if you like; Tiki drinks are not about restraint.

Depending on who you talk to, falernum is a liqueur or a syrup or both. If you're headed to the liquor store, John D. Taylor's Velvet Falernum is a good investment for tiki cocktails. On the syrup side, Fee Brothers and B. G. Reynolds both sell a solid product. It takes some time, but the result is an impressive tidbit to drop into conversations.

Keep It Funky

If you make the Zombie with only one type of rum, it is not a Zombie. Each of the three styles of rum brings a different element to the table: The Jamaican brings the funk, the white rum carries the clean rummy flavors, and the 151 comes in with the proof punch.

CHAPTER 2:

Pretty Drinks

Beauty is always in the eye of the beholder, and love illustrates it and teases it out. Psychological studies also point out that booze makes us think we are more attractive—and that others think we are as well. So, whip up a drink as attractive as you will think you are after it is gone. The drinks in this chapter bring something really pretty to the table, whether it is their hue once mixed, a gorgeous garnish, or even a delicate floral flavor. Check out classics, including the **Whiskey Daisy** (page 115) and the **Daiquiri** (page 104), and more modern beverages, including the **St-Germain Cocktail** (page 112) and **Cosmopolitan** (page 101).

a midday quickie sip

AFTERNOON DELIGHT

—Bartender unknown, J. Bird Cocktails (closed), New York City

A little sweet, a little naughty, and quite boozy, this cocktail pulls together the best of stolen moments for drinking—and other activities. It is a bit of a weird combination, and works best in small batches.

2 ounces gin
½ ounce pear brandy*
¾ ounce fresh lemon juice
¾ ounce fresh orange juice
¾ ounce **Simple Syrup**
(page 212)
Soda water, to top
Orange slice, for garnish

Shake gin, pear brandy, lemon juice, orange juice, simple syrup, and soda with ice. Strain into a chilled Collins glass filled with ice. Top with soda water and garnish with the orange slice.

Pear brandy is fermented and then distilled from pears. Most are sold as eau-de-vies, or unaged fruit brandies. When unaged, it tends to retain much of the character of the original fruit.

hello, beautiful

BELLA BELLA

Beauty may be in the eye of the beholder, but this cocktail is objectively fetching. With citrusy flavors from the Campari, limoncello, orange liqueur, and lime peel twist, it keeps the light, refreshing flavors coming.

1 ounce gin
³/₄ ounces Campari
¹/₂ ounce **Limoncello**
(store-bought or DIY, page 210)
¹/₂ ounce orange liqueur,
such as Cointreau
²/₃ ounces fresh orange juice
Lime peel twist, for garnish*

Shake gin, Campari, limoncello, orange liqueur, and orange juice with ice. Strain into a chilled cocktail glass, and garnish with the lime peel.

*For how to make lime peel twists and other top-notch garnishes, flip to page 216.

"Do I love you because you're beautiful,
Or are you beautiful because I love you?"
—*Rogers & Hammerstein,* Cinderella

APEROL SPRITZ

The Aperol Spritz is one of the simplest—and most iconic—European cocktails. It is also one of the most divisive. People who love it will opine endlessly about its virtues, but its haters are equally as vocal. This beverage is refreshing at any time of day, but the citrusy, bubbly, and complex spritz is the perfect aperitif for just about any meal.

4 ounces prosecco
2 ounces Aperol
$\frac{1}{2}$ to 1 ounce soda water
Orange wedge or lime wheel, to garnish
Straw (optional)

Pour prosecco into a chilled wine glass filled with ice. Follow with Aperol, then top with soda. Garnish with citrus and add a straw, if you please.

join the mile-high club

AVIATION

Even one or two Aviations will have you flying high. This delicate floral cocktail dates back at least to 1911, but despite its crisp floral and citrusy flavors, it was not hugely popular. Its status may have been partially due to crème de violette being hard to find. Luckily, it is easier to find now, and its delicate color and flavor have helped to resurrect this beautiful purple cocktail from the brink of extinction.

2 ounces gin

³/₄ ounce fresh lemon juice

¹/₂ ounce maraschino liqueur, such as Luxardo

¹/₄ ounce crème de violette*

Maraschino cherry, such as Luxardo, for garnish (optional)

Lemon twist, for garnish, (optional)

Shake gin, lemon juice, maraschino liqueur, and crème de violette with ice, and strain into a chilled coupe glass. Garnish as desired.

Crème liqueurs are named for their creamy texture, not any dairy content. This texture comes from the use of a lot of sugar, and any flavoring therein can stem from natural or artificial sources. The best violettes, like Rothman & Winter and The Bitter Truth, are colored and flavored naturally with violet flowers.

peachy keen

BELLINI

It is difficult to overstate how sexy two-ingredient bubbly cocktails can be. They are easily recognizable, but playful and delicious at celebrations typically feted by plain sparkling wine. They are also perfect for brunch time: The booze is softened by the addition of juice or puree like the peach in a Bellini or the crème de cassis in a **Kir Royale** (page 108).

2 ounces fresh peach puree*
4 ounces prosecco
1 fresh peach wedge,
for garnish

Pour peach puree into a flute followed by the prosecco. Stir gently to mix, and garnish with a peach wedge.

A Simple Variation
To make a classic **Mimosa**, substitute orange juice for peach puree and champagne for prosecco. Garnish with a fresh orange wedge (optional).

*Peach puree is available at most grocery stores with the mixers, but can also be made at home. To make it yourself, remove the pits from two peaches, and dice them. Add them to a blender or food processor along with 1 tablespoon lemon juice and 1 teaspoon sugar. Pulse until well-blended, and strain through fine mesh. Discard the solids. Use as soon as possible.

classic dessert drink

BRANDY ALEXANDER

Creamy and sweet, this dessert cocktail is the perfect nightcap for
a date, even if, as Feist sings it, it gets you into trouble. Pair it with
a slice of chocolate cake for a perfectly decadent end to a meal, or
with a couple of strawberries for a lighter option.

1 ounce brandy
1 ounce crème de cacao
1 ounce heavy cream
Pinch of freshly
grated nutmeg

Shake brandy, crème de cacao,
and heavy cream with ice until
well chilled. Strain into a coupe
glass, and grate a dusting of
nutmeg over the surface of the
drink to garnish.

spring is here

CHERRY BLOSSOM COCKTAIL

The blooms of the cherry blossom tree mark the beginning of spring both in Japan and in Washington, D.C. The grenadine's pink hue mimics the blossoms', and the brandy gives it cherry flavor and a bit of a bite—just like the slight lingering chill on that first spring day.

2 ounces brandy

1 ounce cherry brandy

½ ounce dry curaçao

½ ounce **Grenadine** (page 212)*

¾ ounce fresh lemon juice

Maraschino cherry, for garnish

Shake both brandies, curaçao, grenadine, and lemon juice with ice and strain into a chilled cocktail glass. Garnish with the cherry.

For a Crowd

Cherry Blossom Punch: To make this lovely cocktail for a crowd, combine 1 cup brandy, 1 cup cherry brandy, ¼ cup grenadine, ¼ cup dry curaçao, and ⅔ cup lemon juice, and ⅓ cup water in a bowl. Cover and chill in refrigerator before serving. Stir well, and serve over crushed ice. Garnish each with a cherry. *Serves 6.*

Most of the commercially available grenadine is not fit for use in cocktails. It is worth it to spend the time making your own, or investing a bit extra in Jack Rudy, Employees Only, B. G. Reynolds, or Small Hand Foods products.

"Let us be grateful to people who make us happy, they are the charming gardeners who make our souls blossom."

—*Marcel Proust*

not too clichéd

COSMOPOLITAN

For women of a certain age, the Cosmopolitan embodies everything that *Sex and the City* was selling. It is the drink of ladies who power lunch and laugh over their vivacious sex lives. For younger drinkers, it is often a go-to because of its recognizable name. It is valuable for bartenders because drinkers who start with a Cosmo can move further into the world of craft cocktails. Either way, it is a useful tool in any professional or home bartender's arsenal.

2 ounces vodka

1 ounce orange liqueur, such as Cointreau

1 ounce cranberry juice

½ ounce lime juice

½ ounce **Simple Syrup** (page 212)

Lime wheel, for garnish

Shake vodka, orange liqueur, cranberry juice, lime juice, and simple syrup with ice. Strain into either a chilled coupe glass or a chilled Martini glass. Garnish with the lime wheel.

A Simple Variation

For a lovely **Elderflower Cosmopolitan**, substitute white cranberry juice for red, St-Germain for orange liqueur, and lemon juice for lime. Garnish with an edible flower. (Flip to **Floating Flowers**, page 177, for more on bartending with flowers, and **Sources**, page 219, for where to find them.)

CHRYSANTHEMUM

This cocktail is as beautiful as the flower, but with a less cloying scent. It brings together ingredients that do not seem as though they would work on paper, but the result is a super herbaceous tipple.

2 ounces dry vermouth
1 ounce Bénédictine
3 dashes absinthe
Orange twist, for garnish

Stir vermouth, Bénédictine, and absinthe with ice in a mixing glass. Strain into a chilled cocktail glass, and garnish with an orange twist.

bright and dtf (daiquiri time, fool)

DAIQUIRI

The frozen, syrupy sweet concoction that exists under the same name has nothing on its simple, tart predecessor. This easy three-ingredient cocktail revives the elegance of the original to make a drink that is much sexier than artificial store-bought daiquiri mix.

2 ounces rum
³/₄ ounce **Simple Syrup** (page 212)
³/₄ ounce fresh lime juice
Lime wheel, for garnish

Shake rum, simple syrup, and lime juice with ice. Strain into a chilled coupe glass and garnish with a lime wheel.

FLOWER SOURS

Few things are quite as timelessly romantic as flowers. A beautiful bouquet adds class to a simple date and demonstrates thoughtfulness with little effort. Though the effect is slightly different when floral cocktails are in play, the association is largely the same.

In the cocktail world, the Daiquiri is one of a class of cocktail known as a Sour. Typically, these cocktails are comprised of sweet, citrusy, and boozy ingredients. In most classic cocktails, including the Daiquiri, **Gimlet** (page 48), **Bee's Knees** (page 37), whiskey sour, and many others, the main sweetness comes from a syrup and citrusy flavors from juice.

But the simplicity of these cocktails also renders them infinitely customizable. Plain syrups can be swapped out for flavored ones. Even the simplest drinks become elegant with the use of an herbal syrup like lavender or rose petal. Another easy way to incorporate floral elements is to add a dash of flower-flavored bitters like chamomile bitters from 18.21 Bitters, Scrappy's lavender bitters, or Bittercube Bitters's Jamaican #2. To top it off, these modifications also lead to obvious garnishes, like a rose petal, whole flower, or stencil.

why not both?

GIN AND SIN

Perhaps the "sin" part of this cocktail's name refers to the pomegranate in the grenadine, or maybe it is a nod to how delicious this cocktail is. Tempting either way.

2 ounces gin
³/₄ ounce fresh orange juice
¹/₂ ounce fresh lemon juice
¹/₄ ounce **Grenadine** (page 212)

Shake gin, orange juice, lemon juice, and grenadine well with ice and strain into a martini glass.

Most of the commercially available grenadine is not fit for use in cocktails. It is worth it to spend the time making your own, or investing a bit extra in Jack Rudy, Employees Only, B. G. Reynolds, or Small Hand Foods product.

"Between two evils, I always pick
the one I haven't tried before."

—*Mae West*

good morning, beautiful

GOLDEN DAWN

This stout cocktail will awaken your senses and give you a kick
in the pants to get your day started, while the beautiful color will
give you something to contemplate as you sip. Like a sunrise, it is
a wonderful way to wake up during brunch or even as a lunchtime
pick-me-up. Do not be fooled: This complex cocktail is a far cry
from a sickly sweet Tequila Sunrises.

$^3/_4$ ounce Calvados*

$^1/_2$ ounce gin

$^3/_4$ ounce apricot brandy

$^3/_4$ ounce fresh orange juice

Dash of **Grenadine**** (page 212)

Combine calvados, gin, brandy, and
orange juice in a cocktail shaker.
Strain into a chilled cocktail glass,
and dribble the grenadine into the
center of the drink.

*Calvados is an apple brandy produced in Normandy, France. Though it can be made
with a limited amount of pears, most producers avoid their use. Some of it is fiery
eau-de-vie, but like cognac, some products are refined, cask-aged beauties. (**Sources**,
page 219.)

** Most of the commercially available grenadine is not fit for use in cocktails. It is worth
it to spend the time making your own, or investing a bit extra in Jack Rudy, Employees
Only, B. G. Reynolds, or Small Hand Foods products.

"But soft, what light through yonder window breaks?"

—*Shakespeare*, Romeo and Juliet

fancier bubbles

KIR ROYALE

Simple yet fruity and bubbly, the Kir Royale is transformed depending on the quality of the crème de cassis and the dryness of the champagne. When in doubt, purchase the good cassis. And with only two ingredients, it is a perfect cocktail for parties, especially as an after dinner tipple.

¼ ounce crème de cassis*
Cold champagne, to top

Pour cassis into a flute and top with champagne.

A Simple Variation
To make a **Kir,** use flat white wine instead of sparkling.

**Crème de cassis is a crème liqueur, which means it is a black currant liqueur made rich by its sugar content.

a toast

"Vinum regum, rex vinorum."
("Wine of kings, king of wines.")

—*Louis XV*

MÉNAGE À TROIS

There is something that just feels right about ordering a drink that is a little bit naughty. This cocktail is no exception, and the Margarita-like result makes it worth the laughs of ordering. Mix it up during happy hour or dinner to start the romance early.

3 strawberries, and 3 more strawberries reserved for garnish

2 fresh basil leaves, plus 1 more basil leaf reserved for garnish

³/₄ ounce white rum

³/₄ ounce triple sec

¹/₂ ounce fresh lemon juice

¹/₂ ounce gomme syrup*

Place 3 strawberries and 2 fresh basil leaves into the bottom of a mixing glass. Add the rum and crush slightly with a muddler. Add triple sec, lemon juice, gomme syrup, and some ice. Shake vigorously. Strain and pour into a cocktail glass. Garnish with 3 strawberries slices on a swizzle stick, and float the basil leaf on the surface of the drink.

Gomme syrup is nothing more than simple syrup mixed with gum Arabic (or, in the French spelling, gomme Arabic). Gomme syrup can be used in place of simple syrup to give drinks a silkier texture. It is available for sale, but can also be made at home: Gomme Arabic can be purchased at many baking or natural food stores (page 219).

a toast

"There are all types of love in the world, but never the same love twices."

—*F. Scott Fitzgerald*, "The Sensible Thing"

a heavenly elixir

THE VENUS

Named for the goddess of love, this gin cocktail is tinted blush pink with fresh raspberries. The Venus is the color of dawn, the time of the namesake goddess's birth, but its flavors bridges the symbolism of the many areas over which she was goddess.

2 ounces gin

1 ounce Cointreau

¼ ounce **Simple Syrup** (page 212)

Dash of Peychaud's bitters

8 fresh raspberries, with 2 reserved for the garnish

Shake gin, Cointreau, simple syrup, bitters, and 6 of the raspberries vigorously with ice. Strain into a chilled cocktail glass. Garnish with the remaining 2 raspberries on a skewer.

elderflower wisdom

ST-GERMAIN COCKTAIL

It is simple, sweet, and flowery, just like the beginning of many romances. Sip it through summer to cool down or in colder months to remind yourself of the warmth of the sun—it is delicious at any time of year.

2 ounces champagne
1 ½ ounces St-Germain liqueur
2 ounces soda water
Lemon twist, to garnish

Fill a Collins glass with ice. Pour in champagne, St-Germain, and soda water, and stir gently to mix. Garnish with the lemon twist.

sweet as the color or flower

VIOLET FIZZ

Ostensibly named for its color, this cocktail brings together bright summer berry and citrus flavors with gin and a bit of richness. When mixed well, this drink is like an adult raspberry cream soda.

2 ounces London dry gin
½ ounce fresh lemon juice
½ ounce **Raspberry Syrup**
(page 214)
1 teaspoon heavy cream
Soda water, to top
A few raspberries, to garnish

Shake gin, lemon juice, raspberry syrup, and heavy cream. vigorously with ice. Strain into a chilled Collins glass, and top with soda water. Float a raspberry or two on top to garnish.

**Crème de cassis is a crème liqueur, which means it is a black currant liqueur made rich by its sugar content.

"You are the only person who loves me in the world. When you talk to me I smell violets."

—*L. M. Montgomery,* Anne of Windy Poplars

WHISKEY DAISY

The Daisy is a traditional genre of cocktail that originally contained orange liqueur, citrus juice, and booze. But over the years, it evolved to mean a cocktail that contained grenadine, lemon juice, and alcohol. It's still a relatively simple cocktail, but is almost as easy to make as it is to drink.

2 ounces whiskey

1 ounce fresh lemon juice

¼ ounce **Grenadine** (page 212)

¼ ounce **Simple Syrup** (page 212)

Soda water, for topping

Mint or fresh fruit, for garnish

Shake whiskey, lemon juice, grenadine, and simple syrup with ice. Strain into a chilled coupe glass. Top with soda water and garnish with the mint or fresh fruit.

Simple Variations

For a **Gin Daisy**, substitute gin for whiskey. For a **Brandy Daisy**, substitute brandy for whiskey. For a **Tequila Daisy**, substitute tequila for whiskey.

Most of the commercially available grenadine is not fit for use in cocktails. It is worth it to spend the time making your own, or investing a bit extra in Jack Rudy, Employees Only, B. G. Reynolds, or Small Hand Foods products.

CHAPTER 3:

Love Potions

For millennia, humans have ascribed sexual and romantic qualities to many, many foods and animal products. Known as aphrodisiacs, these items have been eaten and drunk to sate hunger while supposedly arousing passion. Many of these items' reputations—like oysters—were originally based on the item's resemblance to human genitalia. Others, like ginger and pepper, are based on the physical sensation that they create when ingested. Although little to no scientific evidence exists to suggest that any specific food items have demonstrable effects on sexual performance, belief in their effects can be just as potent. At least, that is what we have heard. To test it out for yourself, shake up a **Porn Star Martini** (page 132) or **Bourbon Sweetheart** (page 120) if you are feeling sweet, or test out an **Oyster Shell Martini** (page 128) or **Michelada** (page 127) if today calls for something savory.

BOURBON SWEETHEART

This newfangled cocktail is balanced and fizzy enough to sip on a hot summer day, but deep and rich enough to keep on rotation. It is kissable enough to be your sweetheart, but boozy enough to keep you coming back for more.

2 strawberries, sliced, plus one slice reserved for garnish

2 ounces bourbon

½ ounce **Simple Syrup** (page 212)

¼ ounce ginger liqueur

¾ ounce lemon juice

2 dashes aromatic bitters, such as Angostura

Soda water, to top

Muddle the two cut strawberries in a cocktail shaker. Add bourbon, simple syrup, ginger liqueur, lemon juice, bitters, and ice, and shake to combine. Strain into a highball glass full of ice. Top with soda water and garnish with the last strawberry slice perched on the rim of the glass and a straw.

a toast

"Never delay kissing a pretty girl or opening a bottle of whiskey."

—*Ernest Hemingway*

mistakes happen

TRUE LOVE'S SIN

A kiss is not a contract, but a tart drink made with pomegranate juice may just snap you back to your senses. Either that, or the fruit offered in the original temptation might entice you to sin as well.

1 ounce rum
1 ½ ounces
pomegranate juice
¼ ounce **Simple Syrup**
(page 212)
¼ ounce fresh lemon juice
Sparkling wine, to top

Shake rum, pomegranate juice, simple syrup, and lemon juice with ice. Strain into a chilled coupe glass and fill to the brim with wine. Serve immediately.

"Then love is sin, and let me sinful be."
—*John Donne*

damn right I'm a flirt

FLIRTINI

For those effervescent, sweet nights of new romance that beg for a drink of a similar nature, make a Flirtini for your sweetheart. The splash of champagne brings bubbles and crispness, which is balanced by the fruitiness of the other ingredients.

1 ounce vodka
1 ounce pineapple juice
½ ounce orange liqueur, such as Cointreau
Champagne, to top
Maraschino cherry, for garnish

Shake vodka, pineapple juice, and orange liqueur with ice. Strain into a chilled cocktail glass, top with champagne, and garnish with the cherry.

"Love is an irresistible desire to be irresistibly desired."
—*Robert Frost*

to linger a little longer

IRISH COFFEE

If you believe the story, Irish Coffee was originally created to warm up passengers whose flight was turned around due to bad weather in the 1940s. These days, it's even better as a post-meal pick-me-up or even as a liquid dessert on a cold night.

5 to 6 ounces
(³/₄ cup) coffee
2 teaspoons packed
light brown sugar
2 ounces Irish whiskey
Whipped cream,*
for topping

Fill a stemmed, wide-mouthed mug with hot water while coffee brews to warm the mug. Dump out water, and add the sugar and whiskey to the glass along with a small portion of coffee. Stir to combine. Fill mug with coffee to about an inch below the rim. Top with a thick layer of lightly whipped heavy cream.

*For a from-scratch recipe, see page 204.

"I'd rather take coffee than compliments right now."
—*Louisa May Alcott,* Little Women

cool for the summer

STRAWBERRY CAIPIRINHA

Here, Brazil's most famous cocktail gets gussied up with strawberries to go out on the town. The original is a super simple recipe that combines lime, sugar, and cachaça—easy enough to make just about anywhere. The Caipirinha (pronounced kai-pee-reen-ya in Portuguese) has experienced a bit of a Renaissance recently, most likely thanks to its similarity to the **Daiquiri** (page 104). Much like the Daiquiri, it is perfect for sipping on the porch in the summer months, but just as delicious as a reminder of warmer times in front of a fire.

1 lime, quartered
4 strawberry slices, one reserved for garnish
2 ounces cachaça*
½ ounce **Simple Syrup** (page 212)

Muddle lime pieces and three strawberry slices to a pulp with simple syrup in a rocks glass. Add cachaça and ice. Stir well. Cut a slit in the remaining strawberry slice, and perch it on the edge of the glass.

The Original
Omit strawberries and garnish with a lime wheel for a classic **Caipirinha**.

Cachaça is basically the Brazilian take on rum. Very few brands are imported into the United States, but those that make it into the country tend to be funky and slightly weird. Many are sold unaged, but others are aged in casks made from woods not available in the United States. As a whole, cachaça tends to be more similar in production to rhum agricole than the more familiar Spanish-style white rum.

spicy

MICHELADA

Assertive, but still on the lighter ABV side, this traditional Mexican beer cocktail is substantial, refreshing, and can be as spicy as you like. Peppers have long been considered an aphrodisiac since the main spicy compound, capsaicin, stimulates the nerve endings on your tongue to release adrenaline, which also triggers the release of endorphins.

Lime wedge

Tajin,* for rimming

2 ounces fresh lime juice

2 teaspoons Mexican hot sauce, such as Valentina or Tapatío

1 teaspoon Worchestershire sauce

Pinch of salt

12 ounces well chilled Mexican beer, such as Modelo

Use a lime wedge to rim a pint glass with Tajin, and then discard the lime wedge. (See Rimmed Glassware, page 217 for a how-to.) Add lime juice, hot sauce, and Worchestershire sauce except beer to the glass. Fill with ice, and pour in beer. Stir gently to mix. Top up with beer as needed.

*Tajin is a Mexican condiment that brings together chili peppers, salt, and dehydrated lime. For where to find it, see **Sources**, page 219. For a tutorial on rimming cocktail glasses like a bartender, flip to page 217.

"I guess some like it hot.
I personally prefer classical music."

—*1959 romantic comedy,* Some Like It Hot

tastes like the ocean

OYSTER SHELL MARTINI

—Laura Newman, Queen's Park, Birmingham, Alabama

Oysters are possibly the most touted aphrodisiac food. To capitalize on their brine and unique flavor, this cocktail brings together infused vodka, dry vermouth, and sherry for a complex riff on the Dirty Martini.

1 ½ ounces Oyster Shell-Infused Vodka (page 210)

1 ounce dry vermouth, such as Dolin

½ ounce Lustau Manzanilla Sherry

Lemon twist, for garnish

Stir vodka, dry vermouth, and sherry with ice, and strain into a chilled martini glass. Express the lemon twist over top and discard.

PLAN AHEAD

DIY your own Oyster Shell-Infused Vodka at least 24 hours before you need it. See the simple recipe on page 210.

a slurp of the sea

OYSTER SHOOTER

Since the time of the ancient Romans, oysters have been praised
for their near mythical aphrodisiac properties. Kick back these
wonderfully briny shooters as an appetizer or with happy hour nibbles.

1 raw oyster

2 ounces vodka

1 teaspoon **Spicy Cocktail
Sauce** (store-bought or DIY,
page 200)

Lemon wedge

Shuck oyster and drop the meat of it into
a shot glass. Pour in vodka and cocktail
sauce. Squeeze lemon over the glass and
discard the rind. Bottoms up!

A Simple Variation
To make **Sriracha Oyster Shooters,** swap
$^1/_2$ teaspoon sriracha for the cocktail sauce.

**Shucking oysters at home is not as complicated as it might seem. All you need is a
good oyster knife (which you can buy for a couple bucks at your local seafood shop or
cooking store), and a brave attitude. See page 201 for more on selecting and shucking
oysters like a pro.*

BLOODY MARY OYSTER SHOOTER

When a pint glass of Bloody Mary mix is too much and you want something saltier and more petite, mix up a Bloody Mary Oyster Shooter. These work well for lunchtime parties, and can also be served as an accompaniment to a vegetable dish or a savory meat appetizer.

1 fresh raw oyster*
¹/₂ ounce vodka
¹/₂ ounce Bloody Mary mix**
¹/₄ ounce lemon juice
2 drops Tabasco
1 dash Worcestershire sauce
Celery stalk with tip,
for garnish
Lemon wedge, for garnish

Shuck oyster and drop the meat of it into a shot glass. Combine vodka, Bloody Mary mix, lemon juice, and Worcestershire sauce, and pour them into the shot glass. Garnish with the celery stalk and lemon wedge.

*See the footnote on prepping oysters, page 201.
**Plenty of poorly made Bloody Mary mixes are on the market. If you do not have the time or will to make your own, pick up crowd favorites such as Charleston Bloody Mary Mix or the classic Zing Zang. To make it your own, add a couple dashes of your favorite hot sauce or doctor it with your favorite spices. But make sure to taste it before you begin to change it so you have an idea of what you want to do. You can also measure out a cup of it, and doctor that separately before applying your home recipe to the whole bottle.

PORN STAR MARTINI

The name belies the complexity of this drink and the sparkling wine that accompanies it. Though it tends to be on the sweeter side, it has a tropical vibe that is hard to shake.

2 ounces vodka
1 ounce passion fruit puree*
1 ounce **Vanilla Syrup**
(page 214)
½ ounce lime juice
Lime twist or lime wheel,
for garnish
Sidecar of sparkling rosé

Shake vodka, passion fruit puree, vanilla syrup, and lime juice with ice. Strain into a chilled coupe, and garnish with lime. Serve with the sidecar of rosé.

*Passionfruit puree is fairly widely available. If you cannot buy it at your local specialty foods store, it is available frozen or shelf stable from many different sellers on Amazon. (**Sources**, page 219.)*

TWO IS BETTER THAN ONE

A sidecar is a convenient way for serving any
overflow that does not fit in the suggested
glass. But for cocktails such as this, the
ingredient served in the sidecar serves as an
extra measure of refreshment.

spicing things up

SPICY MARGARITA

Some like it hot. Spicy margaritas are perfect for hot nights on porch swings or for heating things up when the weather cools down.

3 jalapeño rounds, 1 or more reserved for garnish

2 ounces tequila

³/₄ ounce triple sec

³/₄ ounce fresh lime juice

Lime wheel, optional

Muddle two jalapeño rounds in a shaker tin. Add tequila, triple sec, and lime juice and ice and shake to combined. Pour into a rocks glass over fresh ice and garnish with additional jalapeño round(s) and lime wheel, if desired.

"He who controls the spice controls the universe."
—*Frank Herbert,* Dune

Put your signature twist on this classic drink. Experiment with **Rimmed Glassware**, *page 217.*

xoxo

THE FRENCH KISS

This classic Valentine's Day tipple combines the richness of white crème de cacao with vodka and chocolate for a concoction you will want to sip deeply.

1 ounce Chambord

1 ounce vodka

1 ounce white crème de cacao

1/2 ounce Cointreau

1 ounce half-and-half

1 chocolate kiss, for garnish,* optional

1 chocolate-dipped raspberry (page 198), optional

Combine Chambord, vodka, white crème de cacao, Cointreau, and half-and-half in a cocktail shaker. Add ice and shake vigorously until chilled, about 15 seconds. Strain into a chilled martini glass and garnish with a chocolate kiss and raspberry if desired.

Simple Variations

Instead of a chocolate kiss, garnish with a white-chocolate kiss or chocolate-dipped raspberry. (For tips on chocolate work, see **Chocolate-Dipped Everything**, page 198.) Or, for a citrusy take, garnish with a twist of orange peel.

To garnish with chocolate kisses: You can simply drop them in the glass, or you can cut a notch into each and perch each one on the rim of the drink.

CHAPTER 4:

Zero-Proof Cocktails

Making sure that your favorite person's needs are met is both mindful and romantic. So, if you or the person you fancy do not drink or need a night off, you may need some non alcoholic recipes in your arsenal that are just as beautiful and delicious.

All of these drinks can be crafted with the same care and attention as any cocktail. To that end, we take care to call them no-ABV (alcohol by volume) cocktails rather than mocktails. They are not fake concoctions, and are a way to make guests at your home or professional bar feel welcomed rather than excluded—or mocked—for their choices. Some of the full-proof cocktails like the **Mexican Hot Chocolate** (page 166), are just as delicious without booze. Within this section, check out the **Blackberry Ginger Fizz** (page 146) or **Lavender Lemonade** (page 148) if you want something citrusy and refreshing, or whip up a **Bitters and Soda** (page 144) if you want something more complex.

drown in love and coffee

AFFOGATO

"Affogato" is Italian for drowned, and after you pour espresso over ice cream, the first rich bite will have you drowning in flavor. For a fancier take, substitute a gelato. Make sure it is one that will complement the coffee notes: typically, one that is creamy and delicious. Anyone who cannot eat dairy can still enjoy an Affogato with a soy, almond, or coconut frozen dessert in place of the traditional ice cream. Do not be afraid make this decadent dessert after a heavy dinner, or even as a mid-afternoon pick-me-up.

2 small scoops vanilla, chocolate, or caramel gelato

1 shot espresso or 3 tablespoons concentrated coffee

Scoop the ice cream or gelato into a bowl. Slowly pour the espresso or coffee overtop. Serve with a spoon.

"I have measured out my life with coffee spoons."
—*T. S. Eliot*

classic and simple

BITTERS AND SODA

This drink is a classic for upset stomachs or as a bitter sipper for when a sweeter beverage will not do. But if you are looking for a 100 percent alcohol-free drink, make sure the bitters you are buying are made with glycerin rather than alcohol.

4 to 10 dashes aromatic bitters, such as Angostura
Soda water, to top

Dash bitters into a Collins glass full of ice. Add soda water, and stir gently with a bar spoon to combine. The soda will fizz up once it comes in contact with the bitters, so pour slowly. For more on bitters, see **Don't Get Bitter**, page 22.

144 *Romantic* Cocktails

THE EARL'S TEA

The bergamot citrus notes in Earl Grey make it easily one of the most accessible—and delicious—teas out there. But on a hot day, it can use some fancying up to take your evening pick-me-up to another level. With the vanilla syrup, this beverage gets a basic, but classy upgrade.

4 ounces freshly brewed
Earl Grey tea
½ ounce fresh lemon juice
½ ounce **Vanilla Syrup**
(page 214)
Soda water, to top
Lavender sprig*

Shake tea, lemon juice, and vanilla syrup with ice. Strain into a chilled Collins glass over fresh ice, and top with soda water. Stir gently to combine, and garnish with the lavender sprig.

*With lavender, a little goes a long way. Too much lavender can taste soapy. So use the sprig mainly to scent the drink as a garnish. Fresh or dried lavender will work. (For where to buy it, see **Sources**, page 219.)

berry nice

BLACKBERRY GINGER FIZZ

Berries are full of vitamin C and other healthful compounds, which are good for the heart and longevity. But if you want to experiment, use blueberries or strawberries—or a combination of the three types of berries.

4 blackberries, plus extra reserved for garnish
1 ½ ounces **Simple Syrup** (page 212), divided
1 ounce fresh lemon juice
Ginger beer, to top
Mint leaf, for garnish

Muddle blackberries in a shaker tin with ½ ounce of the simple syrup. Pour in the rest of the simple syrup and lemon juice and ice. Shake and dump with ice into a Collins glass. Fill glass with ginger beer. Stir gently with a bar spoon and garnish with a blackberry and mint leaf set on top of the ice.

the best of summer

LAVENDER LEMONADE

This drink is easy like a summer afternoon, and a few sips will have you dreaming of porch swings and sunsets breaking over a pristine beach. It is herbal and refreshing, so it is just what you need to keep cool during a long summer night.

1 ½ cups **Lavender Syrup***
(page 212)

1 ½ cups fresh lemon juice

1 cup water

4 lemon wedges, for garnish

4 lavender sprigs, for garnish

Stir lavender syrup, lemon juice, and water together in a pitcher. Chill in the fridge for 45 minutes or until cold. Serve over ice and garnish each glass with a lemon wedge perched on the rim and lavender sprig stuck parallel to the wall of the glass. *Serves 4.*

*The lavender syrup here can be replaced by rose petal syrup, rose hip syrup, violet syrup, rosemary syrup, or another floral, **Botanical Simple Syrup** (page 212). Most of these ingredients are easy to find locally or online, and each of them imparts a distinctive flavor and color to the drink at hand.*

heat it up

SPICY WATERMELON AGUA FRESCA

Bring the spice by combining watermelon and jalapeno for a delightful, richly textured refreshment. This family of drinks is a light, non alcoholic beverage popular in Mexico and the United States that is typically made by blending fruit with water and sugar.

2 cups seedless
watermelon, chopped

2 cups cold water

¼ cup sugar

2 tablespoons
fresh lime juice

½ jalapeño, roughly
chopped

In a blender, combine watermelon, water, sugar, lime juice, and jalapeno. Puree until smooth, and pour into a pitcher. Refrigerate until chilled through, about 2 to 3 hours, or add 1 to 2 cups ice to the pitcher before serving.

A Simple Variation

For a **Spiked Agua Fresca**, shake 5 ounces agua fresca with 1 ½ ounces tequila and ½ ounce fresh lime juice and ice. Strain into a rocks glass over ice, and garnish with a jalapeño round.

bright and spicy

TURMERIC TONIC

Turmeric is in the same family as the ginger plant, and has been used in herbal medicine practices to treat many conditions including pain, fatigue, and breathing issues. In this drink, it is spicy and provides a gorgeous, jewel-tone yellow color, while the ginger and honey help to mellow out this drink.

1 ½ ounces fresh lemon juice
1 ½ ounces **Ginger Honey Syrup** (page 213)
¼ teaspoon ground turmeric
Pinch cayenne

Shake lemon juice, ginger honey syrup, and turmeric in a cocktail shaker with ice. Strain into a chilled rocks glass full of ice. Top with a pinch of cayenne.

CHAPTER 5:

Drinks for Two

As the cliché goes, it takes two to tango. And cocktails for two are easy to make. Most cocktail shakers and mixing glasses are sized to fit at least two drinks, so mix as normal, with a slightly longer shake or stir time to account for the larger volume.

But some recipes, like some people, are meant to come out solo. Before mixing any of the recipes in this section, check in with your boo to make sure that you will both enjoy the drink you make before you invest the extra effort with glassware, ingredients, or prep. If you are going all out with a shared flaming drink like the **Queen of the Lava Beds** (page 168), be sure that your vessel is large enough to hold all of the ingredients and will not shatter or melt if the temperature of the liquid inside changes.

BRIDE'S BOWL

Every wedding party needs a drink for getting ready to help smooth out any road bumps on the big day. Throw together this simple punch the night before, but add the ice and soda water just before serving. For a more highbrow (and slightly boozier) take, substitute sparkling wine for the soda water.

2 (750 mL) bottles aged rum
1 ⅓ cups peach brandy
1 ½ cups unsweetened pineapple juice
½ cup **Simple Syrup** (page 212)
1 cup fresh lemon juice
2 cups fresh pineapple, diced
2 quarts chilled soda water
1 pint strawberries, hulled and sliced

Place rum, brandy, pineapple juice, simple syrup, lemon juice, and pineapple in a punch bowl. Add a block of ice, and just before serving, add soda water and sliced strawberries. To serve, ladle into punch glasses, making sure to add several pieces of fruit. *Serves 20.*

two straws, please

BOOZY MILKSHAKE FOR TWO

It is a classic wholesome rom-com scene: a fresh-faced couple sits on different sides of the diner booth sipping out of a milkshake with two straws. Replicate the moment or make your own memories with your sweetheart with this intoxicating concoction.

2 cups ice cream of your choice, such as caramel

³/₄ cup milk

2 ounces liquor of your choice, such as whiskey

Whipped cream*

Maraschino cherry

Combine ice cream, milk, and booze in a blender. Blend on high speed until smooth, and pour into two smaller glasses or one large glass with two straws. Garnish with whipped cream and a cherry. *Serves 2.*

A Simple Variation

Try adding bourbon to pecan or praline ice cream. Another is adding a splash (or more) of mint liqueur to chocolate ice cream. If you want to get really fancy, you can make **Boozy Ice Cream** (page 195) or add sprinkles or crushed cookies on top as a sweet garnish.

To make your own, see page 204 for a recipe. Variations like Honey Whipped Cream and Cinnamon Whipped Cream make any milkshake extra special.

bubbles for a crowd

CHAMPAGNE PUNCH

If you are hosting a party, chances are you do not want to spend the entire evening behind the bar. Prepare this citrusy, bubbly punch in advance, and have guests serve themselves. To further demonstrate your abilities as a host, create a garnish bar with small labeled glasses of fruit for your guests to use to customize each glass of punch. Though this punch can be served over ice, it does not need to be, as the champagne tones down any booziness and helps to meld all the flavors.

½ cup fresh orange juice

¼ cup fresh lemon juice

½ cup **Simple Syrup** (page 212)

½ cup white rum

½ cup aged rum

1 cup pineapple juice

2 (750 mL) bottles chilled champagne

Cherries, orange slices, or berries, for garnish (optional)

Add orange juice, lemon juice, simple syrup, white rum, aged rum, and pineapple juice to a punch bowl. Stir gently, and place in the fridge to chill. Let sit until chilled through, about 2 to 3 hours. Add champagne immediately before serving. Ladle into punch cups to serve, and garnish with fruit if desired. *Serves 18.*

> "Too much of anything is bad, but too much Champagne is just right."
>
> —*Mark Twain*

FESTIVAL PUNCH

Winter celebrations of any sort are seldom complete without a warm punch. This hot cider variation is mild, but packs a punch for days spent curled up in front of a roaring fire or at gatherings for friends, family, and lovers. If you want to experiment with its flavor, swap out an aged Jamaican rum for a super funky white like Smith & Cross.

4 cups Jamaican rum, such as Appleton Estate

4 cups apple cider

3 cinnamon sticks, broken, plus 8 whole cinnamon sticks, reserved for garnish

2 teaspoons ground allspice

1 tablespoon butter

Heat rum, cider, cinnamon sticks, allspice, and butter in a heavy saucepan over medium heat until almost boiling. Once it is about 195°F, ladle into mugs, straining out broken cinnamon sticks. Garnish with a whole cinnamon stick. *Serves 8.*

"What good is the warmth of summer, without the cold of winter to give it sweetness."

—*John Steinbeck*

steamy

HOT TODDY FOR TWO

Winter is coming, and with it, couples will need a drink to hold while snuggling during movies or sports games. Back before pharmaceutical medicine was widely available, Hot Toddies were often prescribed for colds: the sweetener made the medicine more palatable, the booze relieved pain, spices were thought to have further medicinal qualities, and citrus adds vitamin C. But pretty much everyone has a family recipe for a Hot Toddy, so customize it as much as you like.

1 ounce fresh lemon juice, divided

1 ounce **Honey Syrup,** divided (page 213)

4 ounces bourbon, divided

2 cinnamon sticks

Hot water, for topping

Warm two mugs. (For a quick glass-warming trick, see page 18.) Empty the water, and add half of the lemon juice, half of the honey syrup, and half of the bourbon to each mug. Fill with hot water, and stir to combine. Garnish each with a cinnamon stick.

TEA FOR TWO

Few things are quite as intimate as talking over a shared cup of tea in the afternoon with a loved one. Translate that feeling into a higher-proof tipple with extra herbal notes from the gin and even more depth from the lavender bitters.

2 ounces gin

3/4 ounce **Earl Grey Tea Syrup** (page 212)

3/4 ounces fresh lemon juice

1 dash lavender bitters*

Candied edible flower, for garnish**

Shake gin, tea syrup, juice, and bitters with ice. Strain into a chilled coupe glass, and garnish with an edible flower.

*Lavender bitters are a lovely way to add a bit of floral complexity to a drink, especially with such complementary flavors like the bergamot characteristic of Earl Grey. Some good options include products from Dashfire, Fee Brothers, and Scrappy's.

Flip to **Floating Flowers, page 177, for more information on edible flowers. To find some that are nontoxic and still beautiful, check out the sources on page 219.

"Where there's tea, there's hope."

—*Arthur Wing Pinero*

MEXICAN HOT CHOCOLATE

Few things are quite as romantic as curling up next to your sweetheart next to a fire on a cold night. To add another level of comfort, whip up this spicy, rich hot chocolate to get the blood flowing.

1 ½ cups whole milk

4 ounces high quality semisweet chocolate, finely chopped

1 ½ tablespoons packed brown sugar

½ teaspoon vanilla extract

½ teaspoon ground cinnamon

Pinch of cayenne pepper

Pinch of salt

4 ounces chili liqueur, such as Ancho Reyes

Whipped cream,* for topping

Warm milk in a saucepan over medium heat until steaming. Whisk in chocolate until melted. Bring the mixture to a simmer without letting it boil over. Let simmer, whisking constantly, for 3 to 5 minutes until it thickens. Remove from heat and whisk in brown sugar, vanilla, cinnamon, cayenne, and salt. Pour into two mugs, and add 2 ounces of chili liqueur to each. Top with whipped cream. *Serves 2.*

A Simple Variation
To make **Chartreuse Hot Chocolate**, pour 1½ ounce of Chartreuse into each mug in place of the Ancho Reyes.

If you are in the mood to make Homemade Whipped Cream or—for extra spice— Cinnamon Whipped Cream, see page 204.

Gilding the Lily

For a truly delightful, over-the-top drink, make a batch of **Homemade Marshmallows** (page 202) the night before you plan to serve these. Then float a few in each drink—or perch them on top of the whipped cream.

QUEEN OF THE LAVA BEDS

—Frederic Yarm, Boston, Massachusetts

Worship at the queen's altar by enjoying a bit of fire along with your beverage. This drink, like many other tiki cocktails, packs a punch. Though this tipple for two can be enjoyed solo, the experience is so much more fun with a partner.

2 ounces silver rum, such as Privateer

2 ounces pisco, such as Barsol

1 ounce falernum

1 ounce **Honey Syrup** (page 213)

1 ounce fresh lime juice

1 ounce pineapple juice

2 light dashes aromatic bitters, such as Angostura

2 dashes absinthe, such as St. George

Lime shell and 151-proof rum, to fill

Blend rum, pisco, falernum, honey syrup, lime juice, pineapple juice, bitters, and absinthe with ³/₄ cup crushed ice for 5 to 10 seconds. pour into a 16-ounce Tiki mug, and top with crushed ice. Place a spent half lime shell on the drink's surface, and partially fill it with 151-proof rum. Set the rum in the spent lime shell on fire. Blow out the flame and add a pair of straws before enjoying.

CHAPTER 6:

Modern Craft Cocktails

The craft cocktail resurgence that started more than a decade ago has become a mainstay of drinking culture. It is no surprise, then, that love of all kinds is a big inspiration for drink names and flavor combinations. Where noted, a few cocktails in other sections were created by living bartenders, but this chapter contains the majority of them. From Pride cocktails like the **Off the Wall** (page 185) to funky soon-to-be breakup classics like **I Love You Like a Punch in the Head** (page 178), these drinks will have you tracking down your new favorite bartender. It does not hurt that being able to make contemporary drinks also shows that you are in the know in the craft cocktail loop (**Knowledge Is Sexy**, page 20).

vita brevis, amor eterno

AMOR ETERNO

—*Thomas Reyna, Muldoon's The Patio, Houston*

Life is short, but love endures, just as this drink's name implies.
With a peppery note from the infused tequila and tang from the
balsamic garnish, this drink includes two forms of agave, a plant in
the asparagus family long believed to be an aphrodisiac.

1 ½ ounces **Strawberry and Pink Peppercorn-Infused Tequila** (page 210)

¾ ounce fresh lime juice

½ ounce orange liqueur, such as Cointreau

¼ ounce agave syrup

2 fresh strawberry slices, for garnish

Barrel-aged balsamic vinegar, for garnish

Shake infused tequila, lime juice, orange liqueur, and agave syrup with ice. Strain into a chilled rocks glass full of ice. Garnish with 2 strawberry slices and mist with 2 to 3 sprays of the barrel-aged balsamic vinegar. (For a how-to, see **Misting Your Drinks**, page 215.)

fit for a queen

THE ELENA

—*Sonia Stelea, Esther's Kitchen, Las Vegas*

Rose and ginger add aphrodisiac components to this cocktail, as ginger is believed to increase blood flow while the rose petals add pure romance. Named for the princess of Montenegro to whom the recipe for the liqueur of the same name was gifted, this drink rolls delicate and bold flavors together with a delicious historical background to form a complex and floral cocktail.

1 1/2 ounces spicy rye whiskey, such as High West Double Rye
1/2 ounce Montenegro Amaro
1/4 ounce **Ginger Syrup** (page 213)
10 dashes rose water
Angostura bitters
Bar spoon of amaretto, such as Lazzaroni
1 piece candied ginger, for garnish
Dried 2 to 3 rose petals,*
for garnish

Stir rye, amaro, ginger syrup, bitters, and amaretto well with ice. Strain into a chilled coupe glass. Using a knife, make a small cut in the side of the piece of ginger. Insert the cut side of ginger on to the glass's rim. Float dried rose petals on the surface of the drink.

*The rose petals and other specialty items—like the rose water and rose petals—can be found online (**Sources**, 219) if they are not available at your local grocery store.

it happens to us all, bro

THE FRIEND ZONE
—Markendya Patel, Minnow, Baltimore

If you end up in the Friend Zone, you have probably misread your friend's intentions. To make it a bit more bearable, whip up one of these funky, berry cocktails.

Slice of lime
1 ³/₄ ounces vodka, such as Tito's
1 ³/₄ ounces Brisson Pineau des Charentes*
¹/₄ ounce crème de menthe
¹/₄ ounce raspberry liqueur, such as St. George's
Dried Middle Eastern rose petals**

Muddle lime slice in a cocktail shaker. Add vodka, pineau, crème de menthe, raspberry liqueur, and ice, and shake well. Strain into a rocks glass full of crushed ice and garnish with dried rose petals.

*A Pineau des Charentes, which is also called a **pineau**, is a French fortified wine made by mixing cognac with grape juice. It is available in white and red, but it is not yet well known outside of France.

**For where to find dried edible rose petals, flip to page 219.

FLOATING FLOWERS

Edible flowers are a beautiful—and safe—way to garnish your cocktails. Since many people will try to eat just about anything that is left in their glasses, choosing a flower can be a bit trickier than it might appear on first glance. Some of the best garnishes include violets, pansies, calendula, and hibiscus petals, if you can find them. (For where to order edible blooms, see page 219.)

Simply prepare flowers as you would any produce: Pluck off any blemishes, wash, and pat dry. And note that not all flowers are edible: Some are naturally poisonous, and some (if grown with pesticides or by a roadway) are not good to eat. *Peterson's Field Guide to Edible Wild Plants* is an excellent resource. Whether you grow, forage, or buy your flowers, check that they are USDA organically grown for culinary use.

If you are batching for a party in advance, wait until you are serving the drinks to drop in the flowers: that way, they are less likely to wilt or change its flavors dramatically. Store cut and washed flowers in the refrigerator until you are ready to garnish.

I LOVE YOU LIKE A PUNCH IN THE HEAD

—Beckaly Franks, The Pontiac, Hong Kong

Sometimes, love hurts. Ease the pain with some smoke and herbs. This drink will do just that by bringing together the richness of an egg white with the smokiness of the mezcal and a touch of herbal essence from the Becherovka.

³/₄ ounce tequila

³/₄ ounce mezcal

³/₄ ounce fresh lemon juice

1 teaspoon Becherovka*

¹/₂ ounce **Rich Simple Syrup** (page 214)

¹/₂ ounce egg white (about 1 small egg white)

Bitters, for garnish

Grapefruit twist, for garnish

Shake tequila, mezcal, lemon juice, Becherovka, rich simple syrup, and egg white vigorously without ice. Add ice and shake again. Strain into a chilled coupe glass. Garnish with **Bitters Art** (page 215) and express a grapefruit twist over top. Discard the grapefruit twist.

*Becherovka is a bittersweet herbal liqueur from the Czech Republic. Flavor-wise, it brings a lot of cinnamon, ginger, and clove—kind of like a more mature Fireball.

"Love does not begin and end the way we seem to think it does. Love is a battle, love is a war; love is a growing up."

—James Baldwin

IT'S NOT ME, IT'S YOU

—Christina Mae Henderson, San Francisco, California

A little dry, a little bitter, a little citrusy: just like a breakup.

1 ounce Fernet-Branca
½ ounce dry curaçao, such as Pierre Ferrand
½ ounce sloe gin, such as Sipsmith*
5 dashes Peychaud's bitters
Grapefruit twist, for garnish

Stir fernet, curaçao, sloe gin, and bitters with ice in a mixing glass. Strain into a chilled Old Fashioned glass or small coupe. Express a grapefruit twist over the surface of the drink and drop it in or perch it on the rim.

Sloe gin is not a category of gin, but rather a gin-based liqueur flavored with blackthorn berries, which are nicknamed sloe berries. Unfortunately, they taste horrible on their own, but when steeped in gin with sugar become something delicious.

"For my part, I prefer my heart to be broken. It is so lovely, dawn-kaleidoscopic within the crack."

—D. H. Lawrence

it ties the room together

LARRY'S HOMEWORK

—Shaun Traxler, Vault, Fayetteville, Arkansas

Named for a quote from *The Big Lebowski*, this drink is a very loose play on a White Russian. Thanks to the stimulating effects of the coffee and rich, silky butter-washed rum, Traxler says that this beverage is designed to provide enough energy to love anything or anyone as much as The Dude loves his rug.

1 ounce **Brown Butter-Washed Plantation Original Dark*** (page 210)

½ ounce cognac, such as Pierre Ferrand 1840

½ ounce **Salted Molasses Syrup**** (page 214)

1 ounce cold-brew concentrate

6 dashes mole bitters, such as Bittermen's

Freshly grated nutmeg

Shake butter-washed rum, cognac, salted molasses syrup, cold-brew concentrate, and mole bitters vigorously. Strain into a chilled rocks glass over a stamped ice cube. Garnish with grated nutmeg.

---

*Fat-washing a liquor adds savory flavors—in this case, buttery richness and toasty goodness—to the spirit being modified. It also creates a foam when shaken, much like dairy would in its place.

**Salted caramel is a hugely popular flavor pairing thanks to salt's ability to tone down bitter flavors and caramel's astringent notes. Here, the salt helps to mellow out any of these notes in molasses.

c'mon baby

LIGHT MY FIRE

—*Sam Slaughter, Author of* Grown Up Drinks,
    Greenville, South Carolina

Almost every ingredient in this cocktail is or has been believed
to have aphrodisiac effects. From the agave in the tequila to the
peppers and honey in the syrup, this spicy, sweet, and tart drink
will have you feeling amorous in no time.

1 ½ ounces blanco tequila
³/₄ ounce mango puree
³/₄ ounce fresh lime juice
½ ounce **Habanero Honey Syrup**
(page 213)
Lime zest, for garnish

Shake tequila, mango puree,
lime juice, and syrup well
with ice. Strain into a chilled
cocktail glass, and garnish
with lime zest.

full of contradictions

LONG TALL SHORTY
—*Al Sotack, The Franklin Mortgage & Investment Company, Philadelphia*

This summer sipper brings together watermelon, lemon, and tequila for a refreshing drink that packs a punch. With the little bit of herbal spice from the Cocchi Americano, this drink is perfect for the poolside or a meal outdoors.

1 ½ ounces reposado tequila, such as Espolòn
1 ounce Cocchi Americano*
1 ounce fresh lemon juice
³/₄ ounce **Watermelon Syrup** (page 214)
8 drops jerk bitters**
1 ounce soda water, for topping
Grapefruit twist, for garnish

Shake tequila, Cocchi Americano, lemon juice, watermelon syrup, and jerk bitters with ice. Strain into a Collins draft full of ice cubes, and top with soda. Garnish with the grapefruit twist.

Cocchi Americano is a type of aromatic fortified wine that is infused with herbs and spices. It is flavored with cinchona bark, which adds a slightly bitter, earthy flavor, citrus peel, and other plants to give it a delicate, slightly bitter edge.

**Jerk bitters combine the spices of a Jamaican rub with more bitter flavors, but in cocktails, they tend to add just the slight spice and depth of jerk flavoring. The best known brand of these bitters is The Bitter End's product.*

unique

OFF THE WALL

—Mel Albaladejo, Stonewall Inn, New York

Back in 1969, the Stonewall Inn was the site of riots that launched the gay rights movement. Half a century later, the gay bar is still the site of many monthly community events including drag shows, live music, and, of course, Pride. Mel Albaladejo created this cocktail while listening to Michael Jackson's "Off the Wall," a song that she says captures how she lives her life on her own terms. It's a little bit spicy, a little bit sweet, and a little bit over the top.

2 slices ginger
1 ½ ounces cucumber vodka, such as Stoli Cucumber
½ ounce pomegranate juice
½ ounce fresh lime juice
½ ounce **Simple Syrup** (page 212)
6 grinder shakes white peppercorn
5 mint leaves, 1 reserved for garnish
Cucumber slice, for garnish
1 piece candied ginger, for garnish

Muddle ginger in a shaker tin with vodka, pomegranate juice, lime juice, simple syrup, and white peppercorn. Add mint and ice, then shake until chilled through. Strain into a chilled coupe glass. Garnish by clipping a mint leaf and cucumber slice to the rim of the glass using a tiny clothespin, and perch the candied ginger beside the clip.

ROSE COLORED GLASSES

—Kate Gerwin of Front & Cooper, Santa Cruz, California

This cocktail pairs tropical fruit flavors with a weird, low-proof liqueur (Galliano) and a funky aromatized, floral fortified wine (Lillet Rose). As a whole, it is enjoyably tart, but also brings the funk. If you are making these for a crowd, peel the lemons before juicing them to make the roses in advance. In this case, it may be best to make each drink (or each pair of drinks—just double the recipe) separately to reduce the risk of using too much rose water.

1 ounce Lillet Rose
1 ounce Galliano
1 ounce guava nectar
³/₄ ounce fresh lemon juice
¹/₄ ounce **Honey Syrup**
(page 213)
2 dashes rose water
Citrus peel rose (page 216)

Shake Lillet Rose, Galliano, guava nectar, lemon juice, honey syrup, and rose water well with ice and strain into a Collins glass full of ice. Garnish with the citrus peel rose.

a toast

"Here's to alcohol, the rose colored glasses of life."
—F. Scott Fitzgerald

RYE'N GOSLING

—Julian Goglia, The Mercury, Atlanta, Georgia

This cocktail is almost as sexy as the actor. With some vanilla and peppery spice from the rye, complexity from the rum, and tropical sunshine from the orgeat and lime, it is a great cocktail to sip when you need to daydream about meeting a beautiful person in a beautiful place.

³/₄ ounce rye whiskey

³/₄ ounce dark rum, such as Gosling's

³/₄ ounce orgeat*

³/₄ ounce fresh lime juice

2 dashes Dr. Adam's Aphrodite Bitters

Lime wheel, for garnish

Shake rye, dark rum, orgeat, lime juice, and bitters with ice. Strain into a chilled coupe glass and garnish with a lime wheel and blown kisses.

Orgeat is a tropical syrup made with almond milk, lime zest, and orange flower water. If you want to make it from scratch, check out the recipe on page 214. But Trader Vic's, Small Hand Foods, Giffard, and B. G. Reynolds all make good syrups as well.

CHAPTER 7:

Irresistible Bar Snacks, From-Scratch Ingredients, & Garnishes

Making snacks and cocktail ingredients from scratch can be time-intensive, but it shows that you have put thought into the experience you want to create. As long as nothing is burnt and everything tastes good, it also shows that you have the know-how and skill set to provide for your date regardless of whether the food is pretty or not.

Set the mood with cocktails made with homemade **Grenadine** (page 213) or **Botanical Syrups** (page 212) of your own design, and check out ways to up your **Ice** (page 211) game. Fix some herbed **Snack Crackers** (page 206) to accompany your well-curated **Cheese Board** (page 196), or keep a bowl of **Candied Ginger** (page 209) on hand for some spice. When you are winding down, make sure to have some homemade marshmallows or homemade whipped cream to top your **Mexican Hot Chocolate** (page 166) nightcap. Most importantly, remember to have fun. Making memories is more important than every aspect of the experience being perfect.

Bar Snacks

Romantic food can come in any form. Depending on the couple, even cheap takeout can spark passion. But for newer couples or ones trying to shake it up, a well-curated spread of finger food is perfect. It's not too heavy, but is filling, and is easily abandoned if things get…heated.

A platter of charcuterie, cheese, or fancy olives also pairs with just about any drink. From dark flavors of spirit-forward cocktails like the **Old Fashioned** (page 66) to bubbly **Champagne Cocktails** (page 42), it pairs well, making it wonderful for private moments or a party. To keep things super sexy, make sure that every available nibble is cut so that it would take no more than a bite or two to eat. To that end, we have put together suggestions on making a sexy **Cheese Board** (page 196), **Chocolate-Covered Everything** (page 198), and even **Boozy Marshmallows** (page 203).

two spoons, please

BOOZY ICE CREAM

Just a touch of hooch keeps ice cream a little soft extra scoopable, and adds a tiny bit of grown-up flavor. Substitute it for regular ice cream in a **Boozy Milkshake for Two** (page 158) or up your *Soyer au Champagne* game (page 78).

2 cups milk

2 cups heavy cream

$\frac{1}{2}$ cup sugar

4 large egg yolks

2 tablespoons spirits such as whiskey, limoncello, or Campari*

$\frac{1}{3}$ cup **Simple Syrup** (page 212)

Be careful not to overdo it. Too much booze will make for runny ice cream, because alcohol lowers its freezing point.

In a saucepan over medium heat, warm milk and cream. When the mixture is simmering, stir in sugar, and keep simmering until the granules have dissolved. In a small bowl, whisk yolks with spirits. Slowly whisk half of the steamy milk mixture into the yolk mixture. Then slowly whisk the yolk-milk mixture back into the saucepan. Heat and stir until it thickens and reaches 165ºF. Stir in simple syrup. Strain through a fine-mesh strainer into a 1-quart container. Refrigerate for at least 8 hours or overnight. Process ice cream in an ice-cream maker per the manufacturer's instructions. *Makes 1 quart.*

*You can kick up the alcohol content to about ¼ cup, or even ½ cup for lower alcohol-content drinks, such as wine and beer.

CHEESE BOARDS

For intimate moments, stay away from fragrant cheeses like blue cheese, gruyere, and limburger. However, varying the texture of your choices can help keep the spice alive. Many super salty cheeses are delicious with a touch of honey on a cracker, so find a local honey you like.

Cheese and Cocktail Pairings

Soft, creamy cheeses pair really well with citrusy, bubbly cocktails like the **French 75** (page 46), the **Airmail** (page 34) or the **Champagne Cocktail** (page 42). Baked brie enhances the citrusy notes and some of the softer oak in bourbon, so try it alongside an **Old Fashioned** (page 66). Sharp cheddar plays nicely with just about anything that has some backbone, so serve it up with a rum cocktail like the **Bee's Knees** (page 37) or the **Zombie** (page 86).

Most cheeses and charcuterie taste best at room temperature, so pull them out of the fridge an hour or so before the party starts. Start with 2 to 3 cheeses and 2 to 3 types of meat. To class it up, serve with 1 or 2 types of olives and honey on the side. Make sure to also provide toasted bread or crackers. Generally, ¼ pound of cheese and ⅛ pound of charcuterie will be enough per person, but make sure to adjust that amount based on how much other food will be available.

a chocolate lover's dream come true

CHOCOLATE-DIPPED EVERYTHING

If you are planning out an amorous evening for your sweetheart, few things bring the mood quite like chocolate-dipped morsels. The easiest way to create this effect in advance is to finely chop a 4-ounce bar of semisweet chocolate and microwave it on half power for about a minute, stir, and heat for another minute. Line a pan with parchment paper, and dip pretzels, potato chips, marshmallows, or your favorite berries or other fruits, holding by the stem or one end. When removing it from the chocolate, lift and twist slightly, allowing any excess to fall back into the bowl. Let set for about 30 minutes.

CLASSIC COCKTAIL SAUCE

This spicy, tangy, and slightly sweet condiment is called cocktail sauce for a reason. An essential ingredient in shrimp cocktail and on raw oyster platters, it is tasty when store-bought and even better homemade. Prepare a jar, pick up some fresh oysters and a bottle of vodka, and you are ready to have an **Oyster Shooter** (page 130) party!

1 $2/3$ cups ketchup
$1/3$ cup horseradish
$1/3$ teaspoon fresh lemon juice
$1/2$ teaspoon hot sauce, such as Tapatío or Tabasco
$1/3$ teaspoon freshly ground black pepper
Small pinch of salt, optional

Put ketchup, horseradish, lemon juice, hot sauce, and black pepper in a small bowl. Stir to combine. Taste, and add a small pinch of salt, if desired. Cover and chill in the refrigerator for 30 minutes before serving. Use within 1 to 2 days. *Makes about 2 cups.*

OYSTERS 101

The oyster has had a sexy reputation since at least the Roman Empire. The best oysters—and the ones least likely to make you sick—are the freshest ones. Typically, the local markets that sell oysters will be able to tell you when the bivalves were taken out of the water. They should smell fresh and feel heavy. When you tap them, they should not sound hollow, and the shell should not gape. Once you get them home, throw any with open shells away. Store them in a bowl covered with a wet towel, not with plastic wrap, and do not let them dry out.

When you are ready to prepare them, wash your hands. At this point, it is helpful to have any glassware or plates in place so that you do not have to wash your hands repeatedly. This prep will also guarantee that the oysters will still be super fresh when they are served. Then, scrub the oysters under cold water to remove all potential contaminants or particulates. Wrap a towel over one hand, and hold the oyster securely. Hold your oyster shucking knife in the other hand. Place the tip of the blade into the shell's hinge. Twist the knife while applying pressure to it. Then either use it as a lever upward or continue to twist it to pry open the hinge. Run the knife along the inside of the top shell to separate the meat from the top of the shell, and break open. Then, move the blade under the meat to separate it from the bottom shell.

HOMEMADE MARSHMALLOWS

Cut into thick squares or custom cookie cutter shapes, these DIY marshmallows are a sweet treat. Box them up with a ribbon and gift them, or drop them into mugs of **Mexican Hot Chocolate** (page 166).

2 cups cornstarch
or potato starch

3 cups confectioners' sugar

4 ½ teaspoons unflavored
powdered gelatin

½ cup cold water

¾ cup granulated sugar

½ cup light corn syrup, divided

⅛ teaspoon salt

2 teaspoons pure vanilla extract

Whisk to combine starch and confectioners' sugar, and set aside. Grease an 8-by-8-inch baking pan. In a small bowl, whisk to combine the gelatin and cold water; let soften for 5 minutes. In a saucepan over high heat, stir together the sugar, ¼ cup of the corn syrup, ¼ cup water, and salt. Stir occasionally and let boil until temperature reaches 240°F. Meanwhile, microwave gelatin for 30 seconds or until melted. Pour the remaining ¼ cup corn syrup into the bowl of an electric mixer fitted with the whisk attachment. Mix in the soft, melted gelatin on low speed. When the syrup reaches 240°F, slowly add it the the mixer bowl. Once it has combined, increase the mixer speed to medium and beat for 5 minutes. Then kick it up to medium-high, and beat for 5 minutes more. Finally, beat on the highest setting for 2 more minutes. The finished mallow will be opaque white, and it will have fluffed up to triple in size. Beat in the vanilla extract.

Pour marshmallow into the greased pan, and spread it into the corners. Sift about ½ cup of the starch-confectioners' mixture over top to completely coat. Cover and let cure for 6 hours in a cool, dry place.

Dust a clean work surface with about another $^1/_2$ cup of the starch-confectioners' mixture. Use a knife to loosen the marshmallow from the edges of the pan, and then flip it over onto the work surface. Dust more of the starch-confectioners' mixture on top. Cut into pieces using a knife, a pizza cutter, or cookie cutters for custom shapes. Dip the sticky edges of the marshmallows in more of the starch-confectioners' mixture. Pat off the excess. *Makes about 25 mallows.*

Simple Variations

For a cocktail-inspired treat, try **Boozy Marshmallows**: Use 5 teaspoons gelatin instead of 4 $^1/_2$, and whisk 2 tablespoons 80-proof spirits and $^1/_4$ cup juice in with $^1/_4$ cup cold water instead of $^1/_2$. Then stir in another 2 tablespoons spirits when adding the sugar to the saucepan over high heat.

Put those colors on. To make **Rainbow Marshmallows**, spoon the finished mallow into separate bowls after adding the vanilla extract. Stir a few drops of different colors into each bowl, then layer them in rows in the greased baking pan before curing.

WHIPPED CREAM

Fresh-made whipped cream takes little effort, and it takes every drink and dessert it touches to the next level.

2 cups very cold heavy cream
½ teaspoon vanilla extract
¼ cup confectioners' sugar

Want insurance that your whipped cream will whip up to properly pillowy heights? Chill the mixing bowl in the refrigerator 30 minutes ahead of time.

Pour heavy cream, vanilla, and confectioners' sugar in a large mixing bowl or the bowl of a stand mixer fitted with the whisk attachment. Whip the mixture on high speed for 3 minutes, or until it makes soft, billowy peaks. Serve or cover and refrigerate for up to 4 hours. *Makes about 4 cups (1 quart).*

Simple Variations
For **Honey Whipped Cream,** omit the vanilla and beat in 2 tablespoons **Honey Syrup** (page 213). Raw honey also works, but Honey Syrup blends in extra smoothly.

Irish Coffee, page 124.

SNACK CRACKERS

It is always sexy to be able to casually mention that you have taken the time and effort to make something from scratch. Cut them into shapes that you like (or that will impress your date) or customize the herbs depending on your nights. Use these crackers with a sexy **Cheese Board** (page 196) or dip them in chocolate (page 198). Simple crackers also pair well with just about anything, but try them with a floral **Daiquiri** variation (page 104) or even a **French 75** (page 46) for a really good night.

1 egg

1/3 cup extra-virgin olive oil

2 cups all-purpose flour, plus a few pinches more for dusting

1 teaspoon baking powder

1 teaspoon sugar

1 teaspoon sea salt, plus a few pinches more for topping

1/3 cup ice-cold water

In a small mixing bowl, whisk the egg and olive oil together. In the bowl of a food processor, add 2 cups flour, baking powder, sugar, and salt. Pulse to combine. Add the egg mixture and pulse again, just until crumbs form. Slowly add ice water and pulse until the dough comes together.

Dust a clean work surface and your hands with flour. Plop the dough on it and shape it into two 10-inch squares. Cover them with plastic wrap, and chill in the refrigerator for about 20 minutes.

Preheat oven to 375°F. Grease two baking sheets and dust them with flour. Roll out dough on the dusted work surface until it is about ¼-inch thick. Prick all over with a fork. Scatter salt over top. Cut crackers with a knife, an upside-down shot glass, or cookie cutters, and them place them on baking sheets. (They do not rise, so you can place them fairly close together. Bake for 10 to 15 minutes or until evenly browned. Cover and store for up to 2 weeks at room temperature or up to 3 months in the freezer. (Just give them 1 hour to come to room temperature before serving.) *Makes about 15 dozen snack crackers.*

Simple Variations

Everything Bagel Crackers: For that special someone who is addicted to Trader Joe's Everything but the Bagel Sesame Seasoning Blend (or a similar seasoning mix), omit the salt and instead sprinkle with 2 to 3 teaspoons seasoning mix before baking.

Or, to make **Cheese Crackers**, add 2 to 3 cups shredded cheese to the dough in the food processor, right after adding the ice water. Pulse to combine.

Herbed Crackers: Add about ¼ cup fresh herb leaves to the food processor right after the dough comes together, and pulse briefly to combine.

CUSTOM SHAPES

Cut diamond shapes, letters, hearts, or other shapes with custom-shaped cookie cutters. (For where to find special cutters, see **Sources**, page 219.) You can also freestyle with a knife for a lovely organic look. Just keep all crackers about the same size so that they cook in an even, uniform manner.

From-Scratch Ingredients

Just like with cookies and candy, making ingredients by hand can be an excellent way to put a thoughtful touch on a cocktail or on the experience of a night as a whole. To make things even a little bit sweeter, many of these ingredients take little time and even less effort to make at home. For an easy host or holiday gift idea, bag up extra candy or bottle up syrups or infusions. Print up a homemade tag, and you are set.

CANDIED EVERYTHING

Your honey may be the sweetest thing in your life, so remind them of it with a candied treat. Whether served as a snack on the side or perched on the drink's rim as a garnish, this personalized touch can tie the experience together. Candying things may sound difficult, but it is actually quite simple—much easier than making candy! All you need is a large quantity of sugar, an egg, a paintbrush, and at least a day to let everything dry and cure.

To make stunning **Crystallized Edible Flowers**, gently clean and dry flowers or petals. Brush a thin coating of egg white over the surface of the flower. Gently place each flower in a shallow bowl filled with about 1 cup of superfine sugar. Sprinkle more sugar to coat. Remove from the bowl and place on a piece of waxed paper, sprinkling sugar one more time. Let dry until stiff, about 7 to 8 hours. Store at room temperature in an airtight container.

Candied Ginger is available in bulk at most major health food grocery stores. To make it your own, dip it in chocolate (page 198), or make it yourself. To make it yourself, peel ¹/₂ pound ginger root and slice thinly using a mandolin. Place slices into a saucepan with 2 ¹/₂ cups water over medium-high heat. Cover and cook until ginger is tender, about 35 minutes. Drain ginger through a colander, putting aside ¹/₄ cup of liquid. Weigh ginger, and measure an equivalent amount of sugar. Combine ginger, sugar, and liquid in the saucepan over medium-high heat. Bring to a boil, stirring frequently. Reduce heat to medium, stirring frequently, until the sugar looks dry, is almost gone, and begins to recrystallize, about 20 minutes. Transfer to a drying rack and spread into a thin layer.

INFUSIONS

Infused liquor is a great way to add a personal touch to a classic cocktail or to put a new spin on one. For bars, the matter can be a bit trickier depending on applicable local and state laws, but at home, it can be a great way to demonstrate your creativity.

Brown Butter–Washed Plantation Original Dark

To butter wash the rum, brown 1 stick of butter for each liter of rum you will be fat-washing by melting it in a light-colored pan over medium heat. Keep it cooking evenly by swirling the pan often. The color will begin to darken and reach a toasty brown. Remove the pan for the heat and carefully pour the butter from the pan into a heat-proof bowl. Allow to cool. Combine browned butter with rum, cover, and let sit at room temperature for 8 to 12 hours, shaking frequently. Move to freezer, and let freeze for at least 48 hours. Skim off frozen fat, and strain what remains through a coffee filter.

Limoncello

Peel the zest from 14 lemons, being careful to only remove the yellow part of the skin but not the (bitter) white pith. Place the peels in a one-gallon glass jar. Add 1 ½ liters of 100-proof vodka. Seal and let sit in a cool, dry, dark place for 2 weeks. Do not open the jar during that time. After that two weeks, mix 8 cups of water, and 4 ⅓ cups sugar in a pan, allowing to heat until all of the sugar is dissolved. Strain out the lemon peels from the vodka. Add the sugar solution, and shake slightly to combine. Let rest for 1 month. Then bottle and store in the freezer.

Oyster Shell–Infused Vodka

To infuse vodka, cover one pint cleaned oyster shells with approximately 16 ounces of Ketel One Vodka. Let sit for 24 hours. Fine strain through a cheesecloth-lined chinois strainer.

Strawberry and Pink Peppercorn-Infused Tequila

To make this infused tequila, empty out ¼ of a bottle (about ¾ cup). Insert 1 cup of cut strawberries. Dry pan roast 2 tablespoons of pink peppercorns and pour into bottle.

ICE

Carefully preparing ice can take an ordinary drink and render it into something extraordinary with just a little investment of time and energy. Drinks like the **Old Fashioned** (page 66) can be served over a large cube, a presentation which is made so much sexier with beautiful, clear ice. To up your game, invest in a good set of large cube trays and a couple of spherical molds. (For where to find them, see **Sources**, page 219.)

On their own, the shape will provide a more pleasing aesthetic experience. For less imperfections, boil the water you use or fill the trays with distilled water. To truly up your game, fill a clean hard-sided cooler about halfway with water and freeze overnight, then cut the ice into custom cubes.

Flower-Studded Ice

For an even more decadent experience, fill a spherical mold halfway with ice. Allow to freeze, and add an edible flower. (See **Floating Flowers**, page 177, and **Sources**, page 219.) Alternately, while you are filling up the mold, drop in a few sheets of edible gold leaf, then freeze until solid.

SYRUPS WITH HONEY, HERBS, AND MORE

Making your own syrups at home is as impressive as it is easy. But before we get to the recipes, a note. Syrups are an elementary part of making cocktails, and are made by combining certain ratios of water and sugar. This mixture can be accomplished by measuring either by volume or weight.

Doing it by volume is easier, as it only requires a measuring cup, but mixing syrups by weight is more precise, especially when crafting large batches. It is up to you.

The other big decision before you is whether to heat the sugar with the water or to boil the water separately and add it to the sugar. Typically, the first approach works better for rich simple syrups, while the second is quicker (and more exact) for regular simple syrup. It will be possible to dissolve all of the sugar into hot water in rich syrup, but it may take a bit longer.

There is a reason, after all, that **Simple Syrup** has the name it does. To make it, simply combine one part hot water with one part white sugar and stir until all the sugar is incorporated. Add a teaspoon of vodka for slightly longer shelf life. You can also store syrups in sterilized glass containers to further minimize the introduction of bacteria or other contaminants. *For 1 cup each water and sugar, recipe yields approximately 1 1/2 cups syrup.*

For Botanical Syrups made with delicate flowers or herbs like rose petals or violets, steep 2 cups of fresh edible flowers or 1 cup dried flowers in 1 1/2 cups hot simple syrup for 20 minutes. Strain and store for up to two weeks. *Yields approximately 1 1/2 cups.*

To make a **Lavender Syrup,** mix 2 cups sugar with 2 cups hot water. Once the sugar is dissolved, stir in 1/4 cup of food-grade dried lavender. Cover and chill in the fridge overnight. Strain out the buds, and store for up to two or three weeks. Discard if any cloudiness develops.

To make more robust herbal syrups with hearty herbs like **Rosemary,** make 1 1/2 cups simple syrup. While it's still hot, add 3 long sprigs fresh rosemary. Let steep overnight and strain in the morning, and you have a **Rosemary Syrup** that is exquisite in cocktails as well as baking. *Yields approximately 1 1/2 cups.*

For Cinnamon Syrup, make a simple syrup from 1 cup white sugar and 1 cup boiling water. Stir to combine, and add 3 cinnamon sticks. Let sit for at least 3 hours before straining into a sterilized glass jar. *Yields approximately 1 1/2 cups.*

Demerara Syrup is a rich simple syrup (2:1 ratio of sugar to hot water) made using a less processed sugar like Sugar In The Raw. *Yields approximately 2 cups.*

To make Earl Grey Tea Syrup, brew 1 cup of triple-strength tea using 3 high-quality tea bags or 2 tablespoons loose tea. Cover while steeping to preserve heat. Combine 1 cup strained tea with 2/3 cup white sugar and 1/3 cup packed brown sugar. Stir until all sugar is dissolved.

For Ginger Syrup, combine one large ginger bulb, chopped, 1 quart sugar and 1 ½ quarts water in a saucepan. Heat until the mixture comes to a rolling boil, then cool and let sit for at least 24 hours. Blend mixture, and strain out ginger pulp. Store in fridge. *Yields approximately 1 ¾ quarts.*

For Ginger Honey Syrup, make a **Honey Syrup** with 1 cup honey and 1 cup water (below), and add ½ cup of finely chopped ginger while the syrup is still hot. Let sit for 1 to 2 hours, and strain. Store in a glass jar in the fridge. *Yields approximately 1 ¾ cups.*

Though **Grenadine's** exact origins are unknown, its name comes from "grenade," the French word for pomegranate. Like lime cordial, it was originally made with all-natural ingredients, but with the rise of artificial coloring and flavoring during Prohibition and afterwards, companies found it cheaper to use artificial ingredients rather than natural. With so few people making these ingredients at home, it took the craft cocktail revival to really bring it back.

To make Grenadine, heat one cup pomegranate juice, such as Pom brand, in a saucepan over medium for about five minutes. Add ¾ cup white sugar in a saucepan, and stir until all of the sugar is dissolved. Add 2 tablespoons pomegranate molasses (found at most Middle Eastern markets, or **Sources**, page 219), and cook for about 2 more minutes. Remove from heat and allow to cool to room temperature. Pour into a sterilized glass jar, add 1 teaspoon rosewater, and shake to combine. To store, refrigerate for up to 4 weeks. *Yields approximately 1 ⅓ cups.*

To make Habanero Honey Syrup, bring 1 cup honey and 1 cup water to a boil. Bring down to a simmer and stir until honey is dissolved. Add one diced habanero (with the seeds removed, if desired), and steep for 10 to 15 minutes. Strain and cool before using. *Yields approximately 1 ¾ cups.*

Honey Syrup is simply (pun intended) simple syrup made with honey instead of white sugar, that is to say a ratio of 1:1 honey to water. It is important to note that many varietals of honey exist, and the flavors change depending on the bees' diets. Therefore, the type of honey you use for syrup will directly impact the flavor of the resulting cocktail. *Mixing 1 cup honey with 1 cup boiling water yields approximately 2 cups.*

Orgeat may be the one syrup that is easier and more cost-effective to buy than to make from scratch—if you try to make the almond milk from raw ingredients. Heat 1 cup unsweetened almond milk with 1 cup sugar in a saucepan, and stir to incorporate the sugar. Remove from heat and let cool. Whisk in 2 dashes almond extract and 1 dash rosewater. For a simple variation, swap cashew milk for the almond milk to make a **Cashew Milk Orgeat**. *Yields approximately 1 1/2 cups.*

Raspberry Syrup was used widely in cocktails before **grenadine** came of age. It is a bit sweeter, and a bit more berry-heavy. To make it, smash up 1/2 cup fresh raspberries and mix well with 1 cup sugar. Let the mixture sit for 30 minutes. Add 1/2 cup warm but not hot water, and stir until the sugar has dissolved. Fine strain, and add 1 tablespoon vodka. *Yields approximately 1 1/2 cups.*

Rich Simple Syrup is just as easy, but it is made with a ratio of two parts sugar to one part hot water. It's valuable to note that this ratio of sugar to water will not result in a fully saturated solution, so these ingredients will fully incorporate if shaken or stirred together at room temperature. *Yields approximately 2 cups.*

Salted Molasses Syrup. To make the syrup, combine 1 cup sugar, 1 cup boiling water, 1 tablespoon blackstrap molasses, and one teaspoon kosher salt. Stir until completely dissolved, and allow to cool. *Yields approximately 1 3/4 cups.*

Vanilla Syrup. Make a simple syrup from 1 cup white sugar and 1 cup boiling water. Slice a vanilla bean in half, and scrape out the seeds. Add the seeds and the pod to the syrup. Let sit for at least three hours, then strain into a sterilized glass jar. Store in fridge for up to two weeks. *Yields approximately 1 1/2 cups.*

Watermelon Syrup. To make the watermelon syrup, weigh out 12 ounces of watermelon juice and 12 ounces of sugar. Combine in an airtight container, and shake to combine. *Yields approximately 2 1/4 cups.*

GARNISHES

A garnish serves several purposes. First, it adds a tiny bit of flavor to complete a drink. Citrus peel garnishes add a touch of oil to the drink's aromatics, while cherries give a bit of sweetness to the flavor, and herbal garnishes add to the drink's scent.

Bitters Art is kind of like latte art, except that it is drawn in egg foam with added bitters instead of by carefully pouring textured milk into the mug. There are two ways to make a design: first, by spraying bitters over a stencil onto the foam, or second, by using a dropper to add a few drops, and then using a toothpick or straw to finish the design.

MISTING YOUR DRINKS

Garnishes provide a last tiny hint of flavor that helps to create depth and complete a drink. Misting drinks with balsamic vinegar adds the tiniest bit of savory and tart to balance the agave and liqueur.

An atomizer or other tiny spray bottle is the perfect way to deliver the mist. These containers are available for cheap in bulk on Amazon or at your favorite cooking store, and can be used for balsamic vinegar, absinthe, or any other super flavorful ingredient. To apply, spray once or twice over the surface of the drink.

Candies are a wonderful addition to most beverages if the flavor of the candy complements the flavor of the drink. To use it as a garnish, cut a small cut or notch in the piece of candy and perch it on the rim of the glass.

Citrus fruits are a very traditional way to garnish cocktails. Whether it is a wedge of the fruit or piece of peel, the use of a slice of this type of fruit can add an extra nudge of tartness, while a peel garnish can give citrusy flavor through the expression of its oil.

To express a **peel,** cut a swath of the peel. Direct the colorful side toward the drink's surface, and squeeze the peel to release the oil. You should see a fine mist come off the peel, and a fine layer of the oil on the surface.

To make a **peel** out of roses, cut the zest off of three peels. Roll the peels with the colorful side out into the approximate shape of a rose. Use a toothpick to secure the end of the peel, and run it through the base of the rose to keep the peels in place.

For drinks that require a **spent** lime shell, juice the lime, then push the leftover half back into shape.

A **twist** is the same thing as a peel, but once the peel is expressed, curl the peel around your finger. Drop it into the drink, making sure it keeps its form.

To cut a **wedge**, cut a lemon or lime lengthwise from end to end. Cut that piece in half from end to end, and in half again so that you have eight total slices. To perch it on the rim of a glass, cut a small slit near the middle of the thin end of the slice.

To make a **wheel**, cut the citrus fruit in half crosswise. Make another parallel cut so that you end up with a circular piece that is a cross-section of the fruit. Cut a tiny slit from the rind into the center.

Zesting a fruit just means removing the colorful part of the peel in tiny pieces. Use a zester or a microplane to grate the zest over the surface of the drink.

Edible flowers are a beautiful and classy way to garnish a drink. Use flowers that are as fresh as possible, and wash and dry them as you would other produce. Drop them into drinks at the last possible second to ensure that the flower does not add too much flavor.

Freshly ground spices are a wonderful way to add a touch of darker baking spice flavor to any cocktail. Fresh nutmeg is an especially nutty and delicious addition, especially to drinks like the **Brandy Alexander** (page 99).

Jalapeño rounds are an easy way to add some last minute spice to any beverage.

Traditional **maraschino cherries** were made with tiny, tart Croatian cherries and preserved with liquor and sugar. During Prohibition, companies within the United States began preserving larger, sweeter cherries in chemicals that turned them and their stems a violent red. Cherries add a last touch of sweetness to a drink.

Mint is a beautiful, aromatic garnish for many drinks. Do not reuse leaves you had previously used for muddling as a garnish as they will quickly brown and not add the minty freshness that the drink needs. To make the most of mint, slap it between your palms above the drink to release the oil. This technique is called "spanking."

A leaf can be floated on the surface of a coupe glass or clipped to its rim, or a sprig can be inserted into a straight-walled cup like a Collins or rocks glass next to the straw to ensure its proximity to the straw.

Rimmed glassware is a fun way to add a new flavor component to a beverage by adding salt, sugar, or other spices to its edge. To rim it, wet the rim of the glass with a citrus wedge or a damp sponge. Pour 2 to 3 tablespoons of your rimming material evenly across the surface of a plate. Place the wetted rim of the glass onto the plate, and rotate the glass to capture. Wipe out any excess powder that falls into the glass.

Strawberries can be tricky to use as garnishes. Their shape makes them difficult to perch on the rim of a glass. For most drinks, a cross-sectional slice will be enough and can be floated on the surface of the drink or balanced on its rim.

ABOUT THE AUTHOR AND PHOTOGRAPHER

About the Author

Clair McLafferty is a craft bartender and writer based in Birmingham, Alabama. In 2013, she quit her office job to learn the art of craft bartending after writing about the local scene. Making drinks fed into researching and writing about them, and her current occupation was born. She is the author of *The Classic & Craft Cocktail Recipe Book: The Definitive Guide to Mixing Perfect Cocktails from Aviation to Zombie* (Rockridge Press, 2017) and is the cocktail columnist for *The Bitter Southerner*. For more of her writing, visit clairmclafferty.com.

About the Photographers

Abraham & Susan Rowe are photographers based in Florence, Alabama who work in commercial, documentary, and editorial photography. They offer expertise in photo styling, product, lifestyle and food photography for manufacturing companies, artisans, musicians, e-commerce businesses, and food brands.

Work has been printed in *Elle Decor*, *Local Palate*, *Rolling Stone*, *The National*, *Garden & Gun*, *Southern Living*, *Relix*, *No-Ala Magazine*, and *Business Alabama* as well as online at Kinfolk, Bitter Southerner, Cottage Hill, Local Milk, Paste Magazine, and The New York Times T Magazine.

SOURCES FOR HARD-TO-FIND INGREDIENTS

It does not take much to make a good romantic cocktail. For both classic and obscure home bartending necessities, here are some of the best sources for cocktail ingredients, glassware, and barware.

Bob's Red Mill
A great, widely available brand offering milled grains and a variety of sugars.
BobsRedMill.com

Cocktail Kingdom
Find everything bar-related here: ice trays, shakers, mixing glasses, books, glassware, bitters, and more.
cocktailkingdom.com

Costco
Wholesale source for bulk citrus and sugar.
costco.com

Crate and Barrel
Household goods, including barware, serveware, and glassware.
CrateandBarrel.com

Fantes
Based in the heart of Philadelphia's Italian market, Fantes is a one-stop shop for glassware, barware, ingredients, and everything.
Fantes.com

J. B. Prince
Restaurant wholesaler with glassware and basic bar tools.
JBPrince.com

Kalyustan's
For spices and herbs in midtown Manhattan or online.
FoodsofNations.com.

Koppert Cress
Edible flowers, plants, and other botanicals.
KoppertCress.com

Marx Foods
Edible flowers, produce, and other specialty foods.
MarxFoods.com

Melissa's
Specialty produce.
Melissas.com

MexGrocer
Specialty Latin American products.
Mexgrocer.com

Penzey's Spices
Specialty spices.
Penzeys.com

Sam's Club
Wholesale source for bulk citrus and sugar.
Samsclub.com

Starwest Botanicals
Specialty herbs, teas, essential oils, and spices.
Starwest-Botanicals.com

Sugar Craft
Decorating tools, molds, stencils, sugars, extracts, flower waters, and many other tools and ingredients.
SugarCraft.com

Sur La Table
Household goods, including barware, serveware, and glassware.
SurLaTable.com

Tajin
Spice blend.
tajin.com

Teku
Specialty beer glassware.
TekuGlass.com

Tovolo
Large ice cube trays and other kitchen tools.
Tovolo.com

Valrhona
Specialty chocolate.
Valrhona.com

West Elm
Household goods, including barware, serveware, and glassware.
WestElm.com

Williams-Sonoma
Household goods, including barware, serveware, and glassware.
Williams-Sonoma.com

ACKNOWLEDGMENTS

This book would not have been possible without my community—I am forever grateful for the bartenders, writers, and special humans who have been patient with my endless questions about cocktails and spirits. Even more love and gratitude goes out to all the lovelies who contributed recipes to this book. Y'all are the real MVPs.

When I took on this project, I was going through one of the most difficult seasons of my life to this point: divorce. I joked that, in writing this book, I would rediscover my creative and romantic mojo. The process was only partially successful, but it has taught me how truly incredible the people around me are, especially my former roommates.

Brittany, I am never sure how you do it, but you bring out the best in everyone around you. Mudd and Laura, I am forever grateful for your generosity in taking in me and the (giant) girl dogs and your patience in answering questions and puzzling through recipes at all hours.

There is no way that this book would have gotten finished if it was not for the women who constantly remind me that we are capable and strong and fierce beyond measure, and who do not shy away from the truth. Ingrid, Elba, Sara, Melissa, Carla Jean, Laura, Laura, and all of the rest of you, words do not sum up how much I see and value you.

Mom and Dad, thank you for your support.

Nikki and Tessie, this one is for you, girls. You may be dogs, but you are truly this woman's best friends. Keep the cuddles coming, please.

Finally, *Romantic Cocktails* would not have seen the light of day if it was not for my incredibly patient and long-suffering editor, Margaret McGuire Novak, my publisher John Whalen and Whalen Book Works, not to mention all-star designer Melissa Gerber, proofreader Rebekah Slonim, and the talented Abraham and Susan Rowe of Abraham Rowe Photography. I doubt that I would have written this book without the challenge of having written *The Classic & Craft Cocktail Recipe Book*.

There are certainly people I am forgetting. I love you, and thank you, thank you, thank you.

INDEX

ABOUT WHALEN BOOK WORKS

Whalen Book Works is an independent book publishing company that combines top-notch design, unique formats, and fresh content to create truly innovative gift books. We plant one tree for every 10 books we print, and your purchase supports a tree in the Rocky Mountain National Park.

Visit us on the web at
whalenbooks.com
or write to us at
338 E 100 Street, Suite 5A New York, NY 10029